Software Testing
Advanced Test Analyst
Guide for ISTQB Exam

ISTQB® 2019 Syllabus

First Edition

Catherine Newbould BSc (Hons.) AKC

Software Testing Advanced Test Analyst Guide for ISTQB Exam

First Printing: July 2020

Catherine Newbould BSc (Hons.) AKC
Website: revisionary.co.uk

This book can be ordered online at www.revisionary.co.uk
contact@revisionary.co.uk

Note for Librarians: A cataloguing record for this book is available from
Nielsen Booknet: bookorders.nielsenbooknet.com

ISBN 978-0-9536056-2-0

AiFlex Publishing UK
publish@aiflex.com

About the Author: Catherine Newbould BSc (Hons.) AKC.
With over 25 years of software and systems engineering experience, Catherine Newbould has extensive experience in software testing. Having held senior positions in systems support, computer systems education and management in the United Kingdom, Europe, South Africa and the USA, Catherine's experience ranges from operating systems to general systems testing, defining processes and recommending fixes.

Recent involvement with exam preparation for ISTQB® Foundation and Advanced Test Analyst levels identified a need for a guide aligned to the 2019 ISTQB® Advanced Test Analyst Level certification. The original scope of a book, with a set of exam questions and answers, was extended and developed based on research of the subject. Two complete practice exam papers, each with forty questions and answers aligned to the 2019 Syllabus, are included. These exam papers, along with in-depth descriptions and examples covering decision tables, pairwise testing, orthogonal arrays, test coverage, user stories, use cases and usability techniques, make this publication an essential guide for those wishing to go beyond software testing Foundation Level.

Keywords: Software Testing, ISTQB, Advanced Test Analyst, Test Analyst, Preparation Guide, Practice Paper, Exam, Revision, Syllabus, 2019, 2020, Study Guide, Learning Objective, Knowledge Level, Advanced Level, Test Coverage, Decision Table, Pairwise Testing, Orthogonal Array, Usability, User Story, Use Case.

Disclaimer

In this book many designations, used by organizations to distinguish their products, are claimed as trademarks of their respective companies. Where these designations appear, and AiFlex™ is aware of a trademark claim, designations are acknowledged. All product names and services identified in this book are used in an editorial fashion only and for the benefit of companies, with no intention of infringement of trademarks or other rights. Furthermore, by naming products and services it is not intended to convey endorsement or other affiliation with the company or trademark owner and this book, publisher or its author.

Of particular mention, this book has been written with reference to the International Software Testing Qualifications Board (ISTQB®) 2019 Advanced Test Analyst launch materials. These materials are identified in the *References* Section. The contents of this book and study materials have been created and produced independently. The contents have not been authorised, sponsored or approved by ISTQB or any of its national or international testing boards or subsidiaries, training providers or their affiliates. There is no endorsement or affiliation, expressed or implied, between this book and any organization that prepares or provides training or software testing either in the United Kingdom or internationally.

Certain phrases, themes and context may have been used to align or adhere to the ISTQB® Syllabus.

Every effort has been made to ensure the accuracy of the contents of this book. However, 100% accuracy of the information contained herein cannot be guaranteed. Later versions of ISTQB® documents may result in changes required. While no person can guarantee with certainty that working through any book will result in success in an exam, a studious approach using this book will provide a firm foundation of knowledge on the road to success and achieving certification.

Other materials and updates to the contents may be made available from time to time. Please check at revisionary.co.uk or email contact@revisionary.co.uk.

PREFACE

This book broadens skills and gives practice of software testing techniques. It helps build knowledge and extend understanding to the required level for success in the ISTQB® Advanced Test Analyst exam based on the ISTQB® Syllabus 2019 v1.1 December 19th. The media release of the Syllabus was February 2020. The book should be used with the ISTQB® documents listed in the *References* Section. It assumes ISTQB® Foundation Level has already been achieved and consolidated.

Hints on how to approach the exam, information on particular areas which can be challenging, revision exercises and worked examples based on the 2019 Syllabus are included. The Syllabus is not intended to be a description of the entire knowledge area but it does reflect the level of detail needed. This book has chapters on areas of the Syllabus where additional detail is helpful. The exam practice papers cover the entire Syllabus. Some example questions and answers are extended beyond the Syllabus to meet the demands of the exam. More detail on topics and working around specific areas will assist understanding of the concepts.

Two practice exam papers are included, each covering the full Syllabus. Both practice exam papers have forty original questions in the form and style specified by ISTQB®. Working methodically through the practice questions and understanding how the answers are obtained will provide invaluable help and build confidence ahead of taking the exam.

You are encouraged to make the effort, focus and avoid skipping over any gaps and delve further into relevant materials. It is important to make your learning relevant. Concentrate on the topics and learning which give you marks in the exam. How to achieve this is an aim of this book.

Every software application needs to do what it is designed to do. Your skills in software testing are as important as the designers and software developers and make for a combined team effort. I wish you the very best for your exam preparation, taking the exam and future career.

Once successful in achieving the ISTQB® Advanced Level Test Analyst certification, the door opens to greater opportunities to further a career in software testing and onwards to greater personal achievement. The certification is a significant milestone in any tester's career. Those with ISTQB® Advanced Level Test Analyst certification may use after their name CTAL-TA, Certified Tester Advanced Level – Test Analyst. This official certification is recognized internationally.

If you would like to provide feedback, report inaccuracies or errors, email: contact@revisionary.co.uk
From time to time relevant materials may be added to our website. In addition, errata may be provided where necessary at the revisionary.co.uk website.

Acknowledgement

The Covid-19 lockdown in 2020 has provided the time for writing, reviewing and publishing this book. Our thoughts are with the many families and their friends throughout the world who have tragically lost loved ones or have been otherwise badly affected.

Sincere thanks to both Nigel and Elizabeth Powell CTFL for their help with ideas, proofreading, layout and production as well as encouragement to complete 'the project'. Thanks also to all the students of software testing who are aiming for the Advanced Test Analyst ATA Level certification. Thank you for your support and good luck with your studies.

I acknowledge this book relies on the ISTQB® Advanced Test Analyst Syllabus (2019) and the other documents listed in the *References* Section. This book has been written with compliance to these documents (unless otherwise stated). The Syllabus has been used in accordance with the ISTQB® Syllabus version 2019 V1.1 section 0.1 'Purpose of this Syllabus', sub-point 5 which states the ISTQB® Syllabus is provided, '*to the international software and systems engineering community, to advance the profession of software and systems testing, and as a basis for books and articles.*'

C. N.

Terms Used

In this book, terms have been used as follows:

Syllabus
2019 Launch Document: ISTQB® Certified Tester Advanced Level Syllabus Test Analyst
Version 2019 v1.1 December 19, 2019, from the media release February 2020

Glossary
ISTQB® Standard Glossary of Terms used in Software Testing, version 3.3 November, 2019 and updates to June 2020 where they are known.

Sample Exam / Sample Exam Questions
Sample Exam - Questions ISTQB® Test Analyst Syllabus Advanced Level Exam ID: A Version 2019 1.0

Sample Exam Answers
Sample Exam - Answers ISTQB® Test Analyst Syllabus Advanced Level Exam ID: A Version 2019 1.0

Foundation Level
ISTQB® Foundation Syllabus for Usability Testing Specialist: 2018

These terms have, when it has been deemed useful to do so, been used together with other words from the expanded titles above.

The documents above, together with their locations, are included in the *References* Section at the end of this book.

TABLE OF CONTENTS

Preface vii
Table of Contents 1
Introduction 3
Glossary and Keyword Observations 5
Required Knowledge 9
Knowledge Levels and Learning Objectives 13
Decision Tables 17
Pairwise Testing 37
User Stories and Use Cases 47
Test Coverage 51
Measuring Usability 55
Revision Exercises - Questions 61
Revision Exercises - Answers 71
Checklist for Exam Preparation 79
About the Exam 83
Practice Exam One Questions 91
Practice Exam One Answers 118
Prepare for Practice Exam Two 133
Practice Exam Two Questions 139
Practice Exam Two Answers 166
Booking the Exam 181
References 183
Appendix A: Decision Table Example 186
Appendix B: Using Orthogonal Arrays 190
Quotations 196

INTRODUCTION

This book can be used to extend knowledge of software testing principles. The book is based on the requirements for the ISTQB 2019 Advanced Test Analyst Level. It can also be used to support self-study for the exam or attending a training course. The book should be used in conjunction with the ISTQB launch documents from the media release in February 2020 and the ISTQB Glossary, listed in the *References* Section. Where relevant updates are known, these have been included.

Getting Started
Keep in mind the ISTQB Foundation Level is a prerequisite for the ISTQB Advanced Test Analyst Level, so revise Foundation Level knowledge and terms. For those who have taken the Foundation Level based on the 2012 Syllabus, be aware there are changes and additions to the content and terms for the 2018 Foundation Level. For the Advanced Level, the British Computing Society recommends a minimum of three years of software testing experience before taking the exam.

Use the ISTQB Syllabus 2019
Work through the ISTQB Advanced Test Analyst 2019 Syllabus. The scope of knowledge required is specified in terms of general instructional objectives, referred to as Learning Objectives. These cover terms you need to understand and be able to recall, descriptions of key concepts you need to be able to apply and cognitive learning outcomes that should be achieved.

The Syllabus is not intended to be a description of the entire knowledge area, it reflects the level of detail required. Chapters in this book expand on areas where more detail is particularly useful for answering exam questions and using the techniques in your testing work. If you use other books or sources targeted at the exam, check the information is valid for the 2019 Syllabus or a later version.

Use the ISTQB Glossary
Definitions of terms can be found in the Glossary. The online Glossary is subject to change. More terms than those included in the Advanced Test Analyst Syllabus and for taking the exam are included in the Glossary. For details on using the ISTQB Glossary and where particular attention relevant to the use of techniques or exam requirements is required, see Chapter *Glossary and Keyword Observations.*

Organize Study Time
When allocating study time for the exam, focus on where you will gain marks. Fifty-five percent of the available marks are assigned to questions based on chapter 3 of the Syllabus, *Test Techniques*. Just over thirty percent of the marks are available from questions based on chapter 1, *Tasks in the Test Process* and chapter 4, *Testing Software Quality Characteristics*. For more details of the marks available for particular groups of questions, see Chapter *About the Exam*.

Focus on Learning Objectives

The Learning Objectives are listed in Chapter *Knowledge Levels and Learning Objectives*. Keep referring to these to assess if, with the knowledge and experience you have, you meet these objectives. Questions in the exam are directly linked to the Learning Objectives. Be aware the sub-sections in each chapter of the Syllabus may be, but are not always, numbered in the same way as the Learning Objectives. For example, Learning Objective 4.2.6 is covered in section 4.2.6 while Learning Objective 4.2.5 is covered in section 4.2.4. For the number of questions to expect for a particular Learning Objective, see Chapter *Knowledge Levels and Learning Objectives.*

Understand the K-levels (Knowledge Levels)

Each Learning Objective has an assigned K-level. An exam question may be based on one or more Learning Objectives. The highest K-level is typically considered to be the one assigned to the question. For a more detailed explanation of the K-levels, see Chapter *Knowledge Levels and Learning Objectives.*

Consolidate your knowledge

Allow time to consolidate your knowledge. Everyone learns differently. It is useful to work out what method of consolidation and revision helps you to retain information. It is important to put what you've learned into practice. Use the keywords and terms you encounter in your work and check you are using them correctly. Try out the test techniques. Just staring at your notes or copying them out again is not an effective way to prepare. Try the exercises in Chapter *Revision Exercises*, answers to these are included in the following chapter. A list of hints to use when reviewing your level of knowledge is included in Chapter *Checklist for Exam Preparation*. This will help you create your own tailored revision checklist.

Familiarize yourself with the exam

For those intending to take the exam, understanding the layout of the exam and the format of questions will boost confidence, see Chapter *About the Exam*. The chapter also includes advice on how to approach the exam questions, such as looking for particular words or phrases in the question that affect the answer and how to select the correct answer.

Practice

This book includes two practice exam papers which follow the ISTQB specified exam layout and question formats. Each exam paper contains forty original questions. Use these to check your understanding of concepts and use of techniques or for exam practice. Each paper carries a total of 80 marks, 52 marks are required for a pass. The time allotted for each paper is 120 minutes. Answers are included, together with detailed explanations and working showing how the answers are reached. After completing the first paper, advice is included on how to assess your result and identify the Learning Objectives you should focus on before attempting Practice Exam Two.

GLOSSARY AND KEYWORD OBSERVATIONS

Use the ISTQB Glossary but do not be limited by it. Having a clear understanding of terms is essential for correctly answering exam questions. Answer options in the exam often include an answer that might seem plausible but is incorrect when the strict definitions of terms are applied.

The Glossary can be accessed via the ISTQB website. This online Glossary is subject to change. Glossary v3.3 was the active version at the launch of the 2019 Syllabus. Details of some terms have been changed since the release of the Syllabus and where these are known, they are included in this book. The updates may be included in Glossary v3.4.

Individual terms can be looked up and an advanced search option can be used to provide certain lists, such as keywords for the Advanced Test Analyst Level. A list for the keywords printed from the Glossary before 2020/5/8 should not be used, as it does not correspond to the keywords listed in the Syllabus. A list obtained from the Glossary for non-keyword terms used in Advanced Test Analyst Level should only be used as a rough guide as some terms are in this list but are not in the Syllabus. This may be amended in future. An ISTQB® Glossary Web App User Guide V1.0 is available. See *References* Section for details on accessing the Glossary.

Understanding Terms

Some terms you will know from other contexts as having some variation in meaning or a wider scope from what is required for the exam. For example, you should already be familiar from ISTQB Foundation Level that 'inspection' is defined as '*a type of formal review to identify issues in a work product, which provides measurement to improve the review process and the software development process'* and 'failure' is '*an event in which a component or system does not perform a required function within specified limits*'. In this book, 'inspection' is also used for '*careful scrutiny'*, Oxford English Dictionary definition. Further examples of terms, where you may have a different understanding at the outset, are 'efficiency' and 'effectiveness'. 'Efficiency' refers to '*the degree to which resources are expended in relation to results achieved'*. 'Effectiveness' is '*the extent to which correct and complete goals are achieved'*. With both 'efficiency' and 'effectiveness', functional correctness and functional completeness need to be considered. For details on ways to measure 'efficiency' and 'effectiveness', see Chapter *Measuring Usability*.

The Glossary explains the differences between terms you may consider to be similar in meaning, for example, 'test plan', 'test procedure' and 'test execution schedule'. Another example of the need to understand the difference between terms occurs with 'functional correctness', 'functional completeness' and 'functional appropriateness'. For more information on these terms, see Chapter *Required Knowledge – Quality Characteristics,* page 11.

Some technical terms have very precise Glossary definitions. Some may differ in their detail when compared with definitions from other sources. For example, the Glossary defines the term 'condition' as '*a logical expression that can be evaluated as True or False*'. The ISO 29119 definition for 'condition' has some variation on this, allowing any two values. Other mathematical sources have a different definition which extends the use of the term 'condition' to cover any number of values. This extended definition is used in the ISTQB Sample Exam Answers. For details on the use of the term 'condition', see Chapter *Decision Tables.*

When using the Glossary, make sure you look at the synonyms for some terms, using the expanded detail to display them. For example, the terms 'logical test case' and 'concrete test case' have been removed in the Syllabus, both in the list of keywords required and in the text. 'Logical test case' and 'concrete test case', as applied to test cases, are used in the ISTQB Sample Exam Questions, question #5 and the corresponding answers document. In the Glossary, 'logical test case' is referenced as a synonym of 'high-level test case', 'concrete test case' as a synonym of 'low-level test case'.

Keep in mind some terms that may be used in the Syllabus or exam are not included in the Glossary. A definition for 'round-trip coverage' is not included, 'n-switch coverage' is included. 'Round-trip' applies where sequences of transitions form loops, 'n-switch' refers to the number of switches of length n+1. Other terms needed for the exam that are not in the Glossary include 'satisfaction', see Chapter *Measuring Usability – Satisfaction, and* 'Stakeholder', which is defined in ISO9241-210:2019 as '*the individual or organization having a right, share, claim or interest in a system or in its possession of characteristics that meet their needs and expectations'.*

Also, not in the Glossary is 'parameter-value pair', the combination of a specific parameter with a specific value of the parameter. See Chapter 'Pairwise Testing' for how 'parameter-value pair' is used.

It is important to have an in-depth understanding of the terms used for the quality characteristics and sub-characteristics which define the Test Analyst's responsibilities, see the next table.

To help with exam preparation, keep a list of terms you encounter for which you are initially not confident in being able to recall and learn them.

New Terminology for the Test Analyst's Responsibilities

This table includes terms new in the 2019 Syllabus. It is based on the table from Appendix A of the Syllabus, but with more detail in column three and the amendments listed in notes below the table.

Terms in 2019 Syllabus ISO/IEC 25010	Terms in 2012 Syllabus ISO/IEC 9126-1	Notes on 2019 Syllabus terms in column 1
Functional suitability	Functionality	Expanded to cover two additional sub-characteristics, three sub-characteristics in total
Functional correctness	Accuracy	New term
Functional appropriateness	Suitability	New term
Functional completeness		New definition
	Interoperability	Moved to Compatibility
Usability		Expanded to cover two additional sub-characteristics, six sub-characteristics in total
Appropriateness recognizability	Understandability	New term
Learnability	Learnability	Changed definition in Glossary v3.3 (aligned with ISO 25010)
Operability	Operability	Changed definition in Glossary v3.3 (aligned with ISO 25010)
User error protection		New term. New sub-characteristic
User interface aesthetics	Attractiveness	New term
Accessibility		New sub-characteristic. Changed definition Glossary v3.2†
Portability*		New responsibility, shared with Technical Test Analyst (TTA). Changed definition in Glossary v3.3 (aligned with ISO 25010)
Adaptability*		New responsibility, shared with Technical Test Analyst. Changed definition Glossary v3.3 (aligned with ISO 25010)
Installability*		New responsibility, shared with TTA
Replaceability*		New responsibility, shared with TTA. Changed definition Glossary v3.3
Compatibility**		Release Notes for Glossary v3.2 list this as having a new definition†
Interoperability		Changed definition Glossary v3.2 to align with ISO 25020. See Release Notes Glossary v3.2† No longer synonym of compatibility testing (2020/01/24). Made a keyword 2020/3/7

Notes:

* Additional rows are included for the quality characteristics that a Test Analyst has shared responsibility for with the Technical Test Analyst, as stated in the Syllabus and ISO 25010.

** Co-existence is a sub-characteristic of compatibility but is not included here as it is a responsibility of the Technical Test Analyst (Syllabus).

† Glossary v3.2, April 2018. Other references to Release Notes and Glossary refer to the most recent change being made in Glossary v3.3 November 2019.

Changes in Glossary v3.3

Terminology evolves. The version of the Glossary available at the launch of the 2019 Syllabus is v3.3, November 2019. Details of new terms added, terms changed, terms removed and synonym updates in this version are available in the ISTQB Release Notes v3.3, see *References* Section.

The Release Notes can be useful for checking your knowledge of terms is up-to-date. Use the lists of 'New terms added', 'Terms renamed' and 'Terms changed'. In the latest Release Notes, 'functional correctness' is listed as both a new term and a renamed term, but 'functional appropriateness' which is a new term in the Syllabus, is only listed as a renamed term. Furthermore, 'functional correctness' is listed in 'New terms added' as being aligned to ISO 9126. This ISO standard has been withdrawn. The second occurrence of 'functional correctness' in the 'Terms renamed' refers to the current ISO 25010.

Do not rely on the remarks in the Release Notes for which terms are needed for certification. For example, the remarks for 'New terms added' state 'functional completeness' and 'functional correctness' are used in CTAL TTA (Technical Test Analyst). Be aware these terms are also used in CTAL ATA (Advanced Test Analyst). 'User error protection' is another example of a term marked as used in TTA when it is in ATA.

Terms such as 'embedded iterative model' and 'accessibility testing' have been removed from the Glossary (but not from the Syllabus) as *'defining them does not add any value'* – Release Notes. '*Tester, a person who performs testing'* and other terms with definitions that are straightforward remain. 'n-switch testing' has been removed. The way to refer to this type of testing is, 'state transition testing with n-switch coverage'. 'Test design tool' has been removed from the Glossary with the retirement of the 2012 Syllabus, however it occurs in the 2019 Sample Exam question #40. Keep your knowledge of terms as broad as possible.

If you took the Foundation Level Exam some time ago and learned terminology from before April 2018, you might want to check the changes made to the Glossary that are detailed in the Release Notes for version v3.2, April 2018 and version v3.3, November 2019. Some terms have been renamed, for example, 'test technique' replaces 'test design technique'. However, be aware the term is used in ISTQB launch documents, such as in the ISTQB Sample Exam question #19.

For any queries you may have resulting from reading the Release Notes, check both the Glossary definition and the Syllabus. These have more details for what is required by the Test Analyst. Acronyms are listed in a consistent way in the Glossary and easier to find there. If you need more detail than is provided in the Glossary and Syllabus, use other reputable sources.

Changes since Glossary v3.3

Changes to definitions of keywords have been made for consistency with the Syllabus. Some other terms have been updated to align with ISO definitions or provide clarity. Terms changed can be listed using the advanced search option. This list contains more terms than those used in the Syllabus.

REQUIRED KNOWLEDGE

The Syllabus reflects the level of detail required. It is not a description of the entire knowledge area. Some specific areas, where additional information is beneficial, are covered later in this book.

The 2019 Syllabus has been based on the previous 2012 Syllabus, with some information carried forward, some information changed and some added. There are some omissions in what has been carried forward. For example, the explanation with the answer #5a in the ISTQB Sample Exam Answers references text in the 2012 Syllabus that no longer appears in the 2019 Syllabus. Examples of information changed or added are included later in this book. Having the level of knowledge reflected by the Syllabus will give sufficient understanding to correctly answer questions such as #5.

There is some variation between the ISTQB Syllabus 2019 v1.1 and other current ISTQB downloadable documents. For example, the Syllabus gives a rule for calculating the number of columns in a decision table. The ISTQB Sample Exam Answers use different rules, see Chapter *Decision Tables*. The ISTQB Release Notes Standard Glossary of Terms used in Software Testing v3.3 documents the term 'accessibility testing' is retired with the 2012 Syllabus. The term appears in the Syllabus 2019 v1.1 page 42 and as a distractor in question #26 in the ISTQB Sample Exam. For more information on terms required, changes and amendments, see Chapter *Glossary and Keyword Observations*.

Do not rely on the index at the end of the Syllabus. Some, but not all, of the index entries for keyword terms give only the page number where the keyword is listed and not where there is explanation and discussion of the term. For example, 'accessibility' is given as page 38 when page 42 would be more useful. Similarly, 'test suite' is shown in the index as being on page 10, when page 16 would be more descriptive.

Furthermore, some terms you may need to look up are omitted from the Syllabus index. For example, the term 'appropriateness recognizability', a sub-characteristic of usability, is missing from the index and the list of keywords but is in the Glossary. 'Smoke test' is also not in the index, but is in the Syllabus in three places. The index entry for 'user story testing' shows page 23, *Test Techniques* keywords. This is incorrect as the term was removed from the keyword list in this Syllabus. Many terms in the index are listed twice, once in the singular form, once in plural form. '0-switch' and 'n-switch' are included in the index but not 'round-trip'. There are other inconsistencies with the index. Use the index in conjunction with reading and rereading the Syllabus, until you are familiar with the Syllabus layout. This should mean you have awareness of approximately where in the Syllabus information on a particular term occurs.

It is anticipated that, in later revisions of the ISTQB documents than those available at the time of publication of this edition of the book, inconsistencies will be resolved. Having an in-depth knowledge of the topics in the Syllabus will help you anticipate potential problems. Inconsistencies that are known about are explained in more detail in the relevant sections of this book.

Quality characteristics which can be evaluated by the Test Analyst

The knowledge needed is focused on testing for the quality characteristics which are the responsibility or shared responsibility of the Test Analyst. These characteristics and the questions that should be addressed when evaluating them are included in the table that follows. It is important to understand these characteristics, sub-characteristics and evaluation questions and then be able to apply appropriate processes and techniques as required to test for the characteristics.

Main characteristic followed by sub-characteristics	Evaluating the system or component for the specified characteristic
Functional suitability	Are functions provided that meet the specified and implied needs when used under the specified conditions?
Functional correctness	Are the results correct? Are the results accurate?
Functional appropriateness	Are the functions fulfilled for the users in a way that is considered acceptable?
Functional completeness	Is the specification adhered to? Are all specified functions included?
Usability	Can the intended users achieve the specified goals in the specified context of use?
Appropriateness recognizability	Do the functions facilitate the accomplishment of specified tasks and objectives?
Learnability	Can the intended users, in the specified context of use, achieve specified goals of learning with satisfaction and freedom from risk?
Operability	Are the attributes such that it is easy to operate and control?
User error protection	Are users protected to an acceptable level against making errors?
User interface aesthetics	Does the user interface provide a pleasing and satisfying interaction for the user?
Accessibility	Can users with the widest range of characteristics and capabilities, in the specified context of use, achieve specified goals?
Portability*	Is the transfer from one hardware, software or other operational or usage environment to another, as specified, possible?
Adaptability*	Is this adaptable for different or evolving hardware, software or other operational or usage environments?
Installability*	Can this be installed and/or uninstalled in specified environment(s)?
Replaceability*	Can this replace another component or system for the same purpose in the same environment?
Compatibility†	Can information be exchanged with other components or systems? Can this perform its required functions while sharing the same hardware or software environment?
Interoperability	Can two or more components or systems exchange information and then use the information that has been exchanged?

The characteristics and sub-characteristics above are based on the details in Appendix A of the Syllabus but with the following changes:

* Entries marked with an asterisk have been added. These are quality characteristics that are a shared responsibility with the Technical Test Analyst as in the Syllabus and in ISO 25010, see *References* Section.

† 'Co-existence', a sub-characteristic of 'compatibility', is not included here as this is a responsibility of the Technical Test Analyst.

KNOWLEDGE LEVELS AND LEARNING OBJECTIVES

The Learning Objectives together with their assigned Knowledge level are listed in this chapter in the order of the sections specified in the Syllabus. Learning Objectives are assigned a TA (Test Analyst) reference number.

Knowledge Levels (K-levels)

The K-levels are as below. Questions carry 1, 2 or 3 marks based on their K-level. For details and the number of exam questions at each K-level see Chapter *About the Exam - Where Marks can be Gained or Lost*.

K1 Remember

Definitions of keywords listed at the start of each chapter in the Syllabus should be learned. It is also important to be familiar with additional terms specified for the Advanced Test Analyst Level in the ISTQB Glossary. There are no Learning Objectives at this level. Therefore, no questions in the exam are specifically assigned to K1 level. However, questions at other K-levels will require K1 skills.

K2 Understand

K2 level Learning Objectives require an ability to understand facts, standards and techniques and how they interrelate. This level does not generally require the skills to apply the techniques. Learning Objectives at this level typically start with ‘explain’, ‘summarize the appropriate tasks’, ‘describe’ or ‘define’. The exam regulations state it should be possible to read and answer a K2 exam question in one minute or less.

K3 Apply

K3 level Learning Objectives require the ability to apply facts, techniques and standards but not necessarily how to adapt them or select the most appropriate. Learning Objectives typically start with ‘for a given situation or scenario participate in/determine activities’ or ‘identify problems/tests’. The exam regulations state it should be possible to read and answer a K3 exam question in two minutes.

K4 Analyze

K4 level Learning Objectives require the ability to analyze facts, techniques and standards, apply, adapt as necessary and select the most appropriate. Learning Objectives typically start with ‘analyze’, ‘for a given set of requirements determine which’ or ‘for a given project or scenario select/design’. Most K4 Learning Objectives covering the test techniques were previously at the K3 level in the 2012 Syllabus. The exam regulations state it should be possible to read and answer an exam question at K4 level in three minutes.

Learning Objectives

The list below is set out with:

TA reference number, (K-level), Learning Objective, (number of questions in the exam).

Section 1 The Test Analyst's Tasks in the Test Process

Learning Objectives for the Test Analyst's Tasks in the Test Process

1.1 Introduction

No learning objectives

1.2 Testing in the Software Development Lifecycle

TA-1.2.1 (K2) Explain how and why the timing and level of involvement for the Test Analyst varies when working with different software development lifecycle models. (ONE question)

1.3 Test Analysis

TA-1.3.1 (K2) Summarize the appropriate tasks for the Test Analyst when conducting analysis activities. (ONE question)

1.4 Test Design

TA-1.4.1 (K2) Explain why test conditions should be understood by the stakeholders. (ONE question)

TA-1.4.2 (K4) For a given project scenario, select the appropriate design level for test cases (High-level or Low-level). (TWO questions)

TA-1.4.3 (K2) Explain the issues to be considered in test case design. (NONE or ONE question)

1.5 Test Implementation

TA-1.5.1 (K2) Summarize the appropriate tasks for the Test Analyst when conducting test implementation activities. (NONE or ONE question)

1.6 Test Execution

TA-1.6.1 (K2) Summarize the appropriate tasks for the Test Analyst when conducting test execution activities. (NONE or ONE question)

Section 2 The Test Analysts Tasks in Risk-based Testing

Learning Objectives for The Test Analyst's Tasks in Risk-Based Testing

The Test Analyst's Tasks in Risk-Based Testing

TA-2.1.1 (K3) For a given situation, participate in risk identification, perform risk assessment and propose appropriate risk mitigation. (ONE question)

Section 3 Test Techniques
Learning Objectives for Test Techniques
3.1 Introduction
No learning objectives
3.2 Black-Box Test Techniques
TA-3.2.1 (K4) Analyze a given specification item(s) and design test cases by applying equivalence partitioning. (ONE question)
TA-3.2.2 (K4) Analyze a given specification item(s) and design test cases by applying boundary value analysis. (ONE question)
TA-3.2.3 (K4) Analyze a given specification item(s) and design test cases by applying decision table testing. (TWO questions)
TA-3.2.4 (K4) Analyze a given specification item(s) and design test cases by applying state transition testing. (TWO questions)
TA-3.2.5 (K2) Explain how classification tree diagrams support test techniques. (ONE question)
TA-3.2.6 (K4) Analyze a given specification item(s) and design test cases by applying pairwise testing. (TWO questions)
TA-3.2.7 (K4) Analyze a given specification item(s) and design test cases by applying use case testing. (TWO questions)
TA-3.2.8 (K4) Analyze a system, or its requirement specification, in order to determine likely types of defects to be found and select the appropriate black-box test technique(s). (TWO questions)
3.3 Experience-Based Test Techniques
TA-3.3.1 (K2) Explain the principles of experience-based test techniques and the benefits and drawbacks compared to black-box and defect-based test techniques. (ONE question)
TA-3.3.2 (K3) Identify exploratory tests from a given scenario. (ONE question)
TA-3.3.3 (K2) Describe the application of defect-based test techniques and differentiate their use from black-box test techniques. (ONE question)
3.4 Applying the Most Appropriate Test Techniques
TA-3.4.1 (K4) For a given project situation, determine which black-box or experience-based test techniques should be applied to achieve specific goals. (ONE question)

Section 4 Test Software Quality Characteristics
Learning Objectives for Testing Software Quality Characteristics
4.1 Introduction
No learning objectives
4.2 Quality Characteristics for Business Domain Testing
TA-4.2.1 (K2) Explain what test techniques are appropriate to test the functional completeness, correctness and appropriateness. (ONE or TWO questions)
TA-4.2.2 (K2) Define the typical defects to be targeted for the functional completeness, correctness and appropriateness characteristics. (ONE or TWO questions)
TA-4.2.3 (K2) Define when the functional completeness, correctness and appropriateness characteristics should be tested in the software development lifecycle. (ONE or TWO questions)

TA-4.2.4 (K2) Explain the approaches that would be suitable to verify and validate both the implementation of the usability requirements and the fulfilment of the user's expectations. (ONE or TWO questions)
TA-4.2.5 (K2) Explain the role of the Test Analyst in interoperability testing including identification of the defects to be targeted. (ONE or TWO questions)
TA-4.2.6 (K2) Explain the role of the Test Analyst in portability testing including identification of the defects to be targeted. (ONE or TWO questions)
TA-4.2.7 (K4) For a given set of requirements, determine the test conditions required to verify the functional and/or non-functional quality characteristics within the scope of the Test Analyst. (TWO questions)

Section 5 Reviews
Learning Objectives for Reviews
5.1 Introduction
No learning objectives
5.2 Using Checklists in Reviews
TA-5.2.1 (K3) Identify problems in a requirements specification according to checklist information provided in the Syllabus. (ONE or TWO questions)
TA-5.2.2 (K3) Identify problems in a user story according to checklist information provided in the Syllabus. (ONE or TWO questions)

Section 6 Test Tools and Automation
Learning Objectives for Test Tools and Automation
6.1 Introduction
No learning objectives
6.2 Keyword-Driven Automation
TA-6.2.1 (K3) For a given scenario determine the appropriate activities for a Test Analyst in a keyword-driven automation project. (ONE question)
6.3 Types of Test Tools
TA-6.3.1 (K2) Explain the usage and types of test tools applied in test design, test data preparation and test execution. (ONE question)

DECISION TABLES

The information in this chapter expands on a specific area of the Syllabus where additional detail is useful for answering exam questions and beyond.

The ISTQB Exam Structure and Rules 2019 specifies two mandatory questions for the Learning Objective, '*Analyze a given specification item(s) and designing test cases by applying decision table testing (TA-3.2.3)*'. The two K4 level questions carry a total of 6 marks. An understanding of decision table testing may also be required for other questions such as the K4 question (TA-3.4.1) where you will be asked, '*For a given project situation, determine which test technique should be applied*'.

The K4 level for the decision table testing Learning Objective indicates a required a skill level that includes being able to apply and adapt the technique. To do this competently, study the additional detail and worked examples below.

Essential Definitions

Decision Table - definition from the ISTQB Glossary

'A table used to show sets of conditions and the actions resulting from them'.

Basic Layout of a Decision Table

A decision table is made up of rows and columns across four quadrants:

Conditions being tested	Condition alternatives
Actions to take	Action entries

Conditions are explained in detail later. Actions are associated with decision rules. The associated actions are taken when conditions are met. The number of working columns and rows required is considered later. An additional column is required for the descriptions of the condition rules. Additional rows are required for headings, 'Conditions', 'Actions' and 'Test Case'.

There are two types of decision tables specified in the Syllabus 2019 V1.1. One type covers all combinations of conditions. This type of decision table is often referred to as the 'classic' decision table. For a particular scenario, some of the condition combinations may be redundant or non-feasible. Reducing the complete table to cover only non-redundant and feasible decision combinations is referred to as collapsing the table. The resulting table is called the collapsed table for combinations of conditions.

The second type covers individual condition outcomes. These tables are a new inclusion in the Syllabus. The tables *'ensure that the true and false outcome of each condition is individually tested'*.

A decision table of this type provides a list of test cases where the first column (test case) sets all conditions to their first value, then one condition value is changed in each subsequent column (test case). Non-feasible combinations of conditions can be collapsed.

When creating a decision table of either type, different approaches can be taken depending on the definition (below) and use of the term 'condition'. The Syllabus deals with conditions having one of two values, 'True' or 'False'. Some questions and scenarios may use other definitions.

Condition - definition from the ISTQB Glossary
'A logical expression that can be evaluated as True or False.'

In this book, 'Yes/Y' and 'No/N' are equivalent to 'True' and 'False'.

Condition - definition from ISO 29119
'Boolean expression containing no Boolean operators.
Example: 'A < B' is a condition but 'A and B' is not.'
A condition can have one of two distinct non-dependent values, with no operators linking them.

Condition - definition from Oxford English Dictionary™ OED (and other Mathematical sources)
'Mathematics, etc. The provisions or obligations which an expression or solution is required to fulfil.'

As the OED definition allows for conditions having any number of values, it is inclusive of the ISTQB and ISO definitions which use two-value conditions. The OED definition has more scope to deal with all questions you may encounter as conditions having three or more values are covered.

The ISTQB and ISO definitions of condition can be thought of as aligned to the 'if then else' statement in programming languages, which allows a choice between only two sets of statements. The OED definition allowing for more than two condition values can be thought of as aligned to a case statement. A Dictionary of Computer Science, p72 (see References) defines a case statement as, '*a conditional control structure that appears in most modern programming languages and allows a selection to be made between several sets of program statements. The case statement is a more general structure than the if then else statement.*'

Using the ISTQB or ISO definition, when the OED could be used, will most likely result in additional non-feasible and/or redundant test cases, see example 5. In many scenarios, it is not required or may not be possible to test these additional cases. Full tables for a particular scenario where different definitions of 'condition' could be used, result in the same number of columns in a collapsed table regardless of the definition. Fewer columns are collapsed when using the OED definition. Keep in mind, a greater number of columns adds complexity when deciding which columns to collapse.

To understand the definitions and how to apply them, work through the information in this chapter and study the examples. In many scenarios, there may be more than one correct way to apply the technique.

Decision Tables Covering All Combinations of Conditions

Exam Questions

There are two typical types of exam questions on decision tables covering combinations of conditions.

Type one asks, '*How many test cases are required for minimum coverage of a full/complete decision table covering all combinations of conditions?*' The answer is the number of columns. This number depends on the definition of 'condition' used and if a condition is omitted then assigned later, see below. With different definitions there may be different answers, all are correct for the definition used. There are a few cases when the number will be the same regardless of the definition used.

Keep in mind, when asked for the number of test cases required for a full/complete table, only the number of columns is needed. There is no need to determine the number of rows required.

Type two asks, '*How many test cases are required for minimum coverage of all non-redundant and feasible decision combinations?*' The answer is the number of columns in a collapsed table. To be able to collapse a table, the action rows are required. In a few limited scenarios which may occur in the exam, it may be possible to create a collapsed table from inspection of the scenario, see example 7 on page 29.

Number of columns (test cases) based on the ISTQB and ISO definitions

From the Syllabus:
'The Test Analyst sets up the initial decision table as a complete table where the number of columns is 2 to the power of the number of conditions (2^n where n is the number of conditions). For example, the initial condition table for three conditions would have eight columns or 2^3.'

The above applies when using a definition (ISTQB or ISO) that limits a condition to having one of two values. The statement does not apply when using the OED definition, which is used in the ISTQB Sample Exam Answers, question #10, see example 6 page 27. In some scenarios where conditions are linked, it may be possible to use fewer columns than might otherwise be required, by omitting a condition then assigning it later. This is best explained with a worked scenario, see example 7 (based on ISTQB Sample Exam Question #11) page 29 and *Appendix A*.

Number of columns (test cases) based on the OED definition

Using the OED definition, the total number of columns required in a complete table is equal to the product of the numbers of values of each condition. ISTQB question #10 has condition C3 with four values, C1 and C2 each have two values, the number of columns needed is 16 (4 x 2 x 2).

Number of rows required

The number of rows required is equal to the number of conditions plus the number of actions. Where actions are additive, for example discounts, an additional row may be added to show the outcome of the additive actions such as 'Total discount'.

Steps required to construct a decision table covering all combinations of conditions:

1. Decide which definition of condition to use.
2. Determine the number of condition rules that may affect the decision. The number of condition rules is equal to the number of rows in the top half of the decision table.
3. Calculate the maximum number of columns by multiplying the number of values for each condition. For example, if there are three conditions each with two values, using the ISTQB/ISO definition, 8 (2^3) columns are required. If there are three conditions, two of these conditions have two values each such as 'Y/N' and the third condition has three values such as 'High/Medium/Low', using the OED definition, 12 (2 x 2 x 3) columns are required.

   Stop here for an exam question asking, '*How many test cases are required for minimum coverage of a full/complete decision table covering all combinations of conditions?*'
   The answer is the number of columns.

4. Complete the conditions rows in the top half of the table.

Filling conditions in tables covering combinations of conditions

With three two-value conditions and one action, using the ISTQB/ISO definition, 8 (2^3) working columns and four working rows are required. In the first row, half of the columns have 'Y', half 'N'. In subsequent rows, half of the columns with 'Y' in the row above have 'Y' and the other half have 'N'. Half of the columns with 'N' in the row above have 'Y' and the other half have 'N'.

	Test Case	**1**	**2**	**3**	**4**	**5**	**6**	**7**	**8**
Row	**Condition**								
1	C1	Y	Y	Y	Y	N	N	N	N
2	C2	Y	Y	N	N	Y	Y	N	N
3	C3	Y	N	Y	N	Y	N	Y	N
	Action								
4	A1								

With one condition having three options such as 'High/Medium/Low' (H/M/L) and two conditions having two values such as 'Yes/No' (Y/N), using the OED definition, 12 (3 x 2 x 2) columns are needed. The first row is for the condition having three values, the 12 columns are split into three groups of four columns each. Allow the subsequent rows to be filled with half 'Y', half 'N' as shown.

Test Case	**1**	**2**	**3**	**4**	**5**	**6**	**7**	**8**	**9**	**10**	**11**	**12**
Condition												
C1	H	H	H	H	M	M	M	M	L	L	L	L
C2	Y	Y	N	N	Y	Y	N	N	Y	Y	N	N
C3	Y	N	Y	N	Y	N	Y	N	Y	N	Y	N
Action												
A1												

With two conditions having three options such as 'High/Medium/Low' (H/M/L) and Red/White/Black (R/W/B) such as 'Yes/No' (Y/N), using the OED definition, 9 (3 x 3) columns are required. With one action, three rows are needed.

Test Case	1	2	3	4	5	6	7	8	9
Condition									
C1	H	H	H	M	M	M	L	L	L
C2	R	W	B	R	W	B	R	W	B
Action									
A1									

5. Complete the 'Action' half of the table.

To obtain the collapsed table:

6. For all non-redundant and feasible combinations, replace any condition value that does not affect the outcome with a tilde '~'.
7. Collapse columns where there are non-feasible or redundant combinations

Note: For complex business applications, decision tables can become unmanageable due to a high number of rows and columns. The Test Analyst may consider defining a hierarchy of decision tables. To do this, the conditions of a particular decision table may result in invoking another decision table. This topic is not covered here as it is unlikely a worked example would be required in an exam question.

Questions on Decision Tables covering Combinations of Conditions

Example 1: Using ISTQB definition

A retail company decides to reward its customers with loyalty cards and those placing large orders subject to certain conditions. A customer ordering with a loyalty card has a 5% discount. A customer ordering goods worth more than £50 will have free standard delivery providing delivery is booked for normal business hours. Rewards are additive.

Using decision table testing covering all combinations of conditions, how many test cases are required to cover a full decision table?

a) 6
b) 8
c) 7
d) 5

Select ONE option

Answer

The full table covering all combinations of conditions, based on three conditions, loyalty card, order value and delivery time with two options for each condition, requires 8 (2^3) columns.

b) is the correct answer.

The conditions part of the full decision table:

Test Case	**1**	**2**	**3**	**4**	**5**	**6**	**7**	**8**
Condition								
Loyalty card?	Y	Y	Y	Y	N	N	N	N
Order > £50?	Y	Y	N	N	Y	Y	N	N
Delivery in business hours?	Y	N	Y	N	Y	N	Y	N

Example 2: Collapsing a full/complete table

Consider the same scenario as in example 1. A retail company decides to reward its customers with loyalty cards and those placing large orders subject to certain conditions. A customer ordering with a loyalty card has a 5% discount. A customer ordering goods worth more than £50 will have free standard delivery providing delivery is booked for normal business hours. Rewards are additive.

Using decision table testing covering all combinations of conditions, how many test cases are required to cover all non-redundant and feasible decision rules?

a) 6
b) 8
c) 7
d) 5

Select ONE option

Answer

The full decision table:

Test Case	**1**	**2**	**3**	**4**	**5**	**6**	**7**	**8**
Condition								
Loyalty card?	Y	Y	Y	Y	N	N	N	N
Order > £50?	Y	Y	N	N	Y	Y	N	N
Delivery in business hours?	Y	N	Y	N	Y	N	Y	N
Action								
5% discount	Y	Y	Y	Y	N	N	N	N
Free delivery	Y	N	N	N	Y	N	N	N

If the order is under £50, the delivery charge applies regardless of the delivery time. This means the condition for delivery in business hours in columns 3, 4, 7 and 8 is replaced by a tilde '~'.

Test Case	**1**	**2**	**3**	**4**	**5**	**6**	**7**	**8**
Condition								
Loyalty card?	Y	Y	Y	Y	N	N	N	N
Order > £50?	Y	Y	N	N	Y	Y	N	N
Delivery in business hours?	Y	N	~	~	Y	N	~	~
Action								
5% discount	Y	Y	Y	Y	N	N	N	N
Free delivery	Y	N	N	N	Y	N	N	N

Inspection of the table shows that column 4 can be collapsed into 3 as both columns are similar in condition values and actions. Similarly, column 8 can be collapsed into 7.

Test Case	**1**	**2**	**3**	**5**	**6**	**7**
Condition						
Loyalty card?	Y	Y	Y	N	N	N
Order > £50?	Y	Y	N	Y	Y	N
Delivery in business hours?	Y	N	~	Y	N	~
Action						
5% discount	Y	Y	Y	N	N	N
Free delivery	Y	N	N	Y	N	N

This leaves six columns. One test per column is required so the correct answer is a) 6 test cases.

Example 3: Using the OED definition
Consider the following specification for booking a hotel room.
Staying in a room during the months April to September high-season price applies.
Staying in a room during the months January to March low-season price applies.
At all other times the standard price applies.
Customers with a loyalty card have a 20% discount on the April to December prices.

Using decision table testing covering all combinations of conditions, how many test cases are required to cover all non-redundant and feasible decision rules?

a) 3
b) 8
c) 4
d) 5

Select ONE option

Answer
The first condition, date, has three mutually exclusive options, January to March, April to September and October to December. The second condition is a loyalty card 'Yes' or 'No'. For the decision table, 6 (3 x 2) columns are needed. There are four actions so four rows are needed.

Test Case	**1**	**2**	**3**	**4**	**5**	**6**
Condition						
Date	Jan-Mar	Jan-Mar	Apr-Sept	Apr-Sept	Oct-Dec	Oct-Dec
Loyalty card	Y	N	Y	N	Y	N
Action						
High price	N	N	Y	Y	N	N
Standard price	N	N	N	N	Y	Y
Low price	Y	Y	N	N	N	N
20% discount	N	N	Y	N	Y	N

Looking at columns 1 and 2, the actions result in the same outcome, a low price rate regardless of the condition for a loyalty card so each of these can be replaced by a tilde '~'.

Test Case	**1**	**2**	**3**	**4**	**5**	**6**
Condition						
Date	Jan-Mar	Jan-Mar	Apr-Sept	Apr-Sept	Oct-Dec	Oct-Dec
Loyalty card	~	~	Y	N	Y	N
Action						
High price	N	N	Y	Y	N	N
Standard price	N	N	N	N	Y	Y
Low price	Y	Y	N	N	N	N
20% discount	N	N	Y	N	Y	N

This now makes columns 1 and 2 the same, so they can be collapsed into one column.

Test Case	**1**	**3**	**4**	**5**	**6**
Condition					
Date	Jan-Mar	Apr-Sept	Apr-Sept	Oct-Dec	Oct-Dec
Loyalty card	~	Y	N	Y	N
Action					
High price	N	Y	Y	N	N
Standard price	N	N	N	Y	Y
Low price	Y	N	N	N	N
20% discount	N	Y	N	Y	N

This leaves five columns. One test case for each column is required so the correct answer is d) 5 tests.

Example 4: Using the OED Definition

The following link provides a further example of a decision table with one condition having three options and two conditions having two values so a table of 12 (3 x 2 x 2) columns is used. The example is from a question in the RBCS Software Training and Consultancy Advanced Test Analyst Course – Rex Black. rbcs-us.com/blog/decision-tables-and-testing/

Example 5: Showing the different outcomes depending on the definition of condition
A car is available in two models (Hatchback/Saloon), with two fuel options (Petrol/Diesel) and five paint finishes (Yellow/Red/Silver/Cream/Blue). The price of the car depends on the options selected. The prices (the actions) are not given here as this example focuses on the number of columns required.

For a full decision table covering all combinations of conditions, how many columns (test cases) are required? Use each definition, OED, ISO and ISTQB in turn and compare the answers.

a) 20
b) 32
c) 512
d) 256

Select ONE option

All answers are correct depending on the definition of condition used.

Answer 5 a) Using OED definition with conditions have any number of values:
C1 Car: Hatchback/Saloon
C2 Paint finish: Yellow/Red/Silver/Cream/Blue
C3 Fuel: Petrol/Diesel
Columns (test cases) for all combinations, 20 (2 x 5 x 2)

Answer 5 b) Using ISO definition with conditions having any two values:
C1 Car: Hatchback/Saloon
C2 Paint finish: Yellow/Red
C3 Paint finish: Silver/Cream
C4 Paint finish: Blue Yes/No
C5 Fuel: Petrol/Diesel
Columns (test cases) for all combinations, 32 (2^5).

Answer 5 c) Using ISTQB Glossary definition with conditions having values 'False' or 'True' only.
C1 Car Hatchback: True/False
C2 Car Saloon: True/False
C3 Paint finish Yellow: True/False
C4 Paint finish Red: True/False
C5 Paint finish Silver: True/False
C6 Paint finish: Cream True/False
C7 Paint finish Blue: True/False
C8 Fuel Petrol: True/False
C9 Fuel Diesel: True/False
Columns (test cases) for all combinations, 512 (2^9).

Answer 5 d) Using the ISTQB Glossary definition with conditions having values 'False' or 'True' only and omitting one of the values for paint finish (then assigning the omitted value to columns where there are negatives for the other values of paint finish). Columns (test cases) for all combinations, 256 (2^8). Care needs to be taken when re-assigning any omitted conditions.

Example 6: ISTQB Sample Exam Question #10

'Consider an application that calculates the reimbursements of medical visits for patients having a medical insurance. The medical insurance deductible is defined as the amount of money that the insured patients have to pay before the insurance company begins to pay out benefits. Thus, no charges are reimbursed to the patient until the deductible has been met. There are two types of reimbursable visits: Doctor's Office Visits and Hospital Visits.

The reimbursement for Doctor's Office visits is 33%.

The reimbursement for Hospital visits depends on the type of the specialist visits; four categories (V1, V2, V3, V4) for specialist visits exist and the associated reimbursements are defined as follows:

- *for V1 reimburse 50%*
- *for V2 reimburse 66%*
- *for V3 reimburse 70%*
- *for V4 reimburse 90%*

You decide to model this scenario using a decision table with 3 conditions C1, C2 and C3 where:

C1 can assume two values: Y, N (Y=Deductible met, N=Deductible not met)
C2 can assume two values: D, H (D=Doctor's Office visit, H= Hospital visits)
C3 can assume four values: V1, V2, V3, V4 (categories for specialist visits)

and with 6 actions:

A1 = No reimbursement
A2 = Reimburse 33%
A3 = Reimburse 50%
A4 = Reimburse 66%
A5 = Reimburse 70%
A6 = Reimburse 90%

What is the MINIMUM number of test cases to cover the full decision table?

a) 14
b) 8
c) 6
d) 16

Select ONE option'

Answer

C1 can assume two values: Y, N (Y=Deductible met, N=Deductible not met)
C2 can assume two values: D, H (D=Doctor's Office visit, H= Hospital visits)
C3 can assume four values: V1, V2, V3, V4 (categories for Hospital's specialist visits)

The ISTQB Sample Exam Answers uses the OED definition of condition with C3 having four values. Extract from the ISTQB Sample Exam Answers, *'A full decision table has a number of rules (columns) equal to the product of the numbers of alternative values for each condition. In this case: 2 x 2 x 4 = 16. The minimum test coverage for a decision table is to have one test case for each column of the table: in this case, this means 16 test cases.'*

d) is the correct answer.

The condition part of the full decision table based on the OED definition:

Test Case	**1**	**2**	**3**	**4**	**5**	**6**	**7**	**8**	**9**	**10**	**11**	**12**	**13**	**14**	**15**	**16**
Condition																
Deductible met?	Y	N	Y	N	Y	N	Y	N	Y	N	Y	N	Y	N	Y	N
Doctor(D)/Hospital(H)?	H	H	D	D	H	H	D	D	H	H	D	D	H	H	D	D
V1/V2/V3/V4?	V1	V1			V2	V2			V3	V3			V4	V4		

If the ISO definition of a condition having two values is used, condition C3 can be split into two conditions, a new C3 and C4.

C1 can assume two values: Y, N (Y=Deductible met, N=Deductible not met)
C2 can assume two values: D, H (D=Doctor's Office visit, H=Hospital visit)
C3 can assume two values V1 or V2
C4 can assume two values V3 or V4

With four conditions, each having 2 values, the number of columns required is 16 (2^4). The answer is the same as when using the OED definition. The reason for this is, in this scenario, 2 x 2 x 4 (OED method) is the same as 2^4 (ISO definition method). For a full table covering all condition combinations the answers from different condition definitions may be the same as here, but, depending on the scenario, this will not always be the case, see example 7 on next page.

If the ISTQB definition is used, the conditions are:

C1 can assume two values: Y, N (Y=Deductible met, N=Deductible not met)
C2 can assume two values: Y, N (Y=Doctor's Office visit, N=Hospital visit)
C3: V1 can assume two values: Y, N
C4: V2 can assume two values: Y, N
C5: V3 can assume two values: Y, N
C6: V4 can assume two values: Y, N

The number of columns required here is 64 (2^6). Using the ISTQB method of omitting one condition and later reassigning it results in 32 (2^5) columns. As there are no answer options for these, it should be assumed these methods should not be used here.

Example 7: ISTQB Sample Exam Question #11

'Consider the following specification for a train ticket application:

- *If you want to take a train after 9AM you get the ticket at the "Super-Saver" price.*
- *If you want to take a train before 6AM you get the ticket at a "Saver" price.*
- *At other times of the day you pay the standard price.*
- *If you have a Railcard you get a 25% rebate for all tickets except "Super Saver".*

Using decision table testing, how many test cases are required to cover all non-redundant and feasible decision rules?

a) 3 test cases
b) 8 test cases
c) 4 test cases
d) 5 test cases

Select ONE option'

Answer

d) is the correct answer. Five test cases are required for all feasible and non-redundant decision rules.

Using OED Definition

Condition 1: Three possible ticket types, Before 6am, 6am to 9am and after 9am.
Condition 2: Railcard Yes/No

Using the OED definition, a full decision table has 6 (3 x 2) columns. This collapses to 5 columns for feasible and non-redundant decision rules. (*Appendix A*).

Using Inspection

From the scenario, it can be seen by inspection that the non-redundant and feasible test cases required are:

1. Before 6am, Saver with Railcard
2. Before 6am, Saver, no Railcard
3. Between 6am and 9am, Standard with Railcard
4. Between 6am and 9am, Standard, no Railcard
5. After 9am, Super-Saver

Using ISTQB definition

When conditions are only allowed to have Yes or No values, the conditions can be defined:

Condition 1: ticket type, Before 6am, Yes/No
Condition 2: ticket type, 6am to 9am, Yes/No
Condition 3: ticket type, after 9am, Yes/No
Condition 4: Railcard, Yes/No

A full decision table has 16 (2^4) columns. This collapses to 5 columns for feasible and non-redundant decision rules. (*Appendix A*).

Adapting the ISTQB definition / used in the ISTQB Sample Answers

Condition 1: ticket type, Before 6am, Yes/No
Condition 2: ticket type, after 9am. Yes/No
Condition 3: Railcard Yes/No

This results in a non-collapsed decision table with 8 (2^3) columns. Two of the decision rules are together not feasible because the conditions, after 9am and before 6am cannot both be true. This reduces the number of decision rules to 6. Two columns where condition 1 and condition 2 are both 'N' are reassigned the ticket type 6am to 9am. As the price of this type of ticket is not discounted by having a Railcard, the two columns are collapsed into one. This results in a collapsed table with five columns. (*Appendix A*).

BEWARE This method of omitting a condition value can be used here because the effect of having a Railcard is linked to having a ticket. There is no valid action for having a Railcard without a ticket. However, consider a scenario where a user can park at the train station for a pickup or other reason. If this replaces Railcard, the third condition is 'Car Parking Yes/No', with a discount on a ticket if purchased. It is now no longer possible to reassign the two columns as it is valid to park with no train ticket. So, if using the method of reassigning columns, be certain the conditions are not fully independent of each other.

For the full and collapsed decision tables for answering this question, see *Appendix A: Decision Table Example*.

BEWARE If question #11 had asked the same question as in question #10, *'What is the MINIMUM number of test cases to cover the full decision table?'*, there are three correct answers 6, 8 or 16, depending on the definition of 'condition' used, see above.

Decision Tables Covering Individual Condition Outcomes

Decision tables covering individual outcomes are a new addition to the Syllabus. For a scenario, where conditions have two values, all are set to their first value in column one and then, one condition at a time is set to its second value in the subsequent columns. The stated objective of this approach in the Syllabus is, '*to ensure that the true and false outcome of each condition is individually tested*'. However, the method can be used for scenarios where there are conditions with more than two values. This extends the objective above to ensure that every value of every condition is individually tested.

There are no questions in the ISTQB Sample Exam on this type of decision table but there may be questions in the exam. Questions on this type of decision table are included in the practice exam papers in this book.

The Syllabus explains, *'Since each decision rule focuses on a specific condition, the localization of any defects revealed is simplified'.* In many scenarios this is true but not always, see example 9. The Syllabus states, *'defects that occur only when certain combinations of conditions exist may be missed since only simple combinations are considered'.* Note the inclusion of the word 'may'. This type of defect can be missed, but this is not always true. Consideration of this is also in example 9.

In scenarios where, one condition with its 'Yes' value overrides all other decision rules and its 'No' value does not affect the decision (or vice versa), consider removing this condition from the table and then adding one extra test case for the of the omitted condition having the value that overrides the other decision rules. This alternative method is explained at the end of example 9. Consider applying this technique to the scenario in ISTQB Sample Exam question #10. Using 'not met' for the first value of the condition, 'Deductible' will show similar limitations to those in example 9.

Number of rows required

The number of rows required in a decision table covering individual condition outcomes is equal to the number of conditions and actions, the number does not include the rows where the words, 'Conditions' and 'Actions' occur. Where actions may be additive, for example discounts, an additional row may be added to show the outcome of the additive actions such as 'Total discount', see example 9.

Number of columns (test cases) required

1. Using the ISTQB/ISO definitions of conditions having only two values, the number of columns required in the decision table is the number of conditions plus 1. For example, with three two-value conditions, four columns are required as follows:

Test Case	**1**	**2**	**3**	**4**
Condition				
C1	Y	N	Y	Y
C2	Y	Y	N	Y
C3	Y	Y	Y	N
Action				
A1				

2. Using the OED definition of condition, the number of columns required for a decision table covering individual condition outcomes where one condition has three values and two conditions have two values is 5. For example, C1 can have values 'High/Medium/Low' (H/M/L), C2 and C3 are either 'Y' or 'N'. All individual conditions are included in a table with five columns.

Test Case	**1**	**2**	**3**	**4**	**5**
Condition					
C1	H	M	L	H	H
C2	Y	Y	Y	N	Y
C3	Y	Y	Y	Y	N
Action					
A1					

The ISTQB Syllabus method for calculating the number of rows only works for scenarios where conditions have two values. For all scenarios where decision tables covering individual condition outcomes are required and conditions may have any number of values, use the equation below. Set condition C1 to be the condition with the greatest number of values, v_1.

$$\text{Number of Columns} = v_1 + \sum_{i=2}^{N} (v_i - 1)$$

N = number of conditions

v_1 = number of values for the condition C having the greatest number of values

v_i = number of values for condition C_i

For the scenarios above:

1. $N = 3$, $v_1 = 2$, $v_2 - 1 = 1$, $v_3 - 1 = 1$
Number of columns = 2 + 1 + 1 = 4

2. $N = 3$, $v_1 = 3$, $v_2 - 1 = 1$, $v_3 - 1 = 1$
Number of columns = 3 + 1 + 1 = 5

Questions on Decision Tables covering Individual Condition Outcomes

Example 8: Using the OED definition

Consider the scenario in example 5, page 26. A car comes in two models (Hatchback/Saloon), with two fuel options (Petrol/Diesel) and five paint finishes (Yellow/Red/Silver/Cream/Blue). The price of the car depends on the options selected. The prices (actions) are not given here as this example focuses on the number of columns required.

For a decision table covering individual condition outcomes, how many columns (test cases) are required?

a) 3
b) 4
c) 7
d) 8

Select ONE option

Answer

C1 Car: Hatchback/Saloon
C2 Paint finish: Yellow/Red/Silver/Cream/Blue
C3 Fuel: Petrol/Diesel

Seven (5 for each of the paint finishes plus 2, the number of conditions with 2 values) columns (test cases) are required. C2 is set to Yellow (first value) and then changed to its other values in columns 2 to 5. In column 6, C2 is reset to Yellow and C1 is changed to its second value. In column 7, C1 is reset to its first value and C3 is changed to its second value. All individual conditions are tested by the table below:

Test Case	**1**	**2**	**3**	**4**	**5**	**6**	**7**
Condition							
C1	Hatch	Hatch	Hatch	Hatch	Hatch	Saloon	Hatch
C2	Yellow	Red	Silver	Cream	Blue	Yellow	Yellow
C3	Petrol	Petrol	Petrol	Petrol	Petrol	Petrol	Diesel

c) is the correct answer.

Example 9: Limitations of decision table covering individual outcomes

You are working on an application for a computer equipment supply company. The company wishes to give discounts. Customers with a loyalty card receive 2% discount. All orders completed online automatically receive an extra 3% discount. Discounts are additive. Special orders (for example software installation) are exempt from discounting. You are reviewing testing with a decision table using all individual condition outcomes.

Using a decision table covering individual outcomes for this scenario, which option is the most true?

a) Four test cases are indicated and there is simplification of localization of defects as there are separate test cases for each discount applied
b) Six test cases are indicated, two of which are non-feasible. The four remaining test cases cover no discount, 2% discount, 3% discount and 5% (2% + 3%) discount
c) Changing the initial condition values to 'No' does not change the number of test cases indicated or the overall test case outcomes. Both discounts are tested individually and together
d) The test cases cover all individual condition outcomes but not all specified result outcomes for the user

Select ONE option

Answer

Using conditions having only two values, with three conditions (payment with loyalty card, online ordering, special order), 4 (2 + 2) columns are required. (Two for the first condition which has two values plus two, the number of remaining conditions having two values).

Setting all values initially to 'Yes'

Test Case	**1**	**2**	**3**	**4**
Condition				
Loyalty card?	Y	N	Y	Y
Online?	Y	Y	N	Y
Special order?	Y	Y	Y	N
Action				
2% discount				Y
3% discount				Y
0% discount	Y	Y	Y	N
Total % discount	0	0	0	5

When no overall discount applies, the actions for other discounts do not apply so are left blank. The table includes a test case where both discounts apply. Simplification of the localisation of any defects, should they occur with applying only one discount is not achieved, making a) not correct.

Using inspection, testing individual conditions could be amended to testing available discounts by changing the 'Special order' row as shown below:

Test Case	**1**	**2**	**3**	**4**
Condition				
Loyalty card?	~	N	Y	Y
Online?	~	Y	N	Y
Special order?	Y	**N**	**N**	N
Action				
2% discount			Y	Y
3% discount		Y	N	Y
0% discount	Y	N	N	N
Total % discount	0	3	2	5

This now shows test cases for all available discounts but this is now a table testing individual result outcomes and six tests are not required. This makes b) incorrect.

Setting all values initially to 'No'

Test Case	**1**	**2**	**3**	**4**
Condition				
Loyalty card?	N	Y	N	N
Online?	N	N	Y	N
Special order?	N	N	N	Y
Action				
2% discount	N	Y	N	
3% discount	N	N	Y	
0% discount	N	N	N	Y
Total % discount	0	2	3	0

This table covers all individual values of conditions, so localization of defects, should they occur, is simplified. Test cases do not have the same combinations as when values are initially set to 'Yes'. If there is a defect in calculating the discount when two discounts apply, this will not be discovered with this set of test cases. This makes c) not correct.

The correct answer is d). See the table on page 34.

Alternative Method

Construct the individual condition outcomes table without the condition for 'Special order'. This leaves 2 conditions (Loyalty card and Online) each with 2 values, and the number of columns required is now 3 (2 + 1). This is found from the first condition having 2 values and there being 1 additional two value condition.

Test Case	**1**	**2**	**3**
Condition			
Loyalty card?	Y	N	Y
Online?	Y	Y	N
Action			
2% discount	Y	N	Y
3% discount	Y	Y	N
Total % discount	5	3	2

Then add an additional test for 'Special order'.

Test Case	**1**	**2**	**3**	**4**
Condition				
Loyalty card?	Y	N	Y	~
Online?	Y	Y	N	~
Special Order?	N	N	N	Y
Action				
2% discount	Y	N	Y	
3% discount	Y	Y	N	
0% discount	N	N	N	Y
Total % discount	5	3	2	0

This also results in four test cases with all discounts possible being covered.

Note: Whilst the above methods result in four test cases, the test cases are different. The quality of the set of four test cases can be variable depending on the method used to construct a decision table covering individual outcomes. The Test Analyst should assess the best method for the particular scenario.

PAIRWISE TESTING

The information in this chapter expands on a specific area of the Syllabus where additional detail is useful for answering exam questions and beyond.

The ISTQB Exam Structure and Rules 2019 specifies two mandatory questions for the Learning Objective, *'Analyze a given specification and designing test cases by applying pairwise testing' (TA-3.2.6).* The two questions are both at K4 level, so carry a total of 6 marks. An understanding of pairwise testing may also be required for the K4 question (TA-3.4.1), where you are asked to determine which test technique should be applied.

The K4 level indicates a requirement that includes being able to apply and adapt the technique. To do this competently, additional detail to that available in the Syllabus is required. The Syllabus recommends a tool is used. In scenarios with a large number of parameters and parameter-value pairs, pairwise testing can become complex and a tool will be useful. Understanding and being able to apply basic principles of pairwise testing is essential for answering exam questions. A manual approach illustrates the principles. Some exam questions that require an answer for the number of test cases required are likely to be based on scenarios with a small number of parameters and parameter pairs. This is where a manual approach may work well and in the exam is the method available. Understanding the limitations of the manual approach will help identify the scenarios where the manual method is not appropriate. Advice on how to deal with more complex scenarios is described later in this chapter.

The term 'pairwise testing' has an updated definition in the ISTQB Glossary v3.3 and now includes the term 'parameter-value pairs'. The definition of pairwise testing is '*a black-box test technique in which test cases are designed to exercise pairs of parameter-value pairs.* A 'parameter-value pair' is a name and a value used to identify the data value. For example, if a parameter is 'payment' and has four values; VISA™, MasterCard™, PayPal™, and bank transfer, there are four parameter-value pairs; payment-VISA, payment-MasterCard, payment-PayPal and payment-bank transfer.

Pairwise testing uses combinatorial arithmetic to test every parameter-value pair of a parameter with every parameter-value pair from all other parameters. While keeping the testing quality at a high level, the technique reduces the overall number of test cases that might otherwise be needed as several pairs are tested in a test case.

An initial pairwise table is based on the assumption the input parameters have values that can be combined with any value of other parameters. Where there are non-feasible pairs, first build a table without this requirement, then inspect the table and adjust for or remove non-feasible pairs.

Exam Questions on Pairwise Testing

A typical exam question may ask for the minimum number of pairwise test cases required for a particular scenario. The number of rows needed for a pairwise table equals the number of test cases required. Other typical questions may ask about the steps involved in setting up a pairwise table or to review a given pairwise table.

Calculating the guideline minimum number of rows is shown below. This number, in some scenarios, may equal the actual number of rows required, but this is not always true. Additional rows are often needed. It is advisable to be aware of and be able to recall scenarios where the guideline minimum number of rows does not equal the number of actual rows needed. Working out the actual number of rows can be done using orthogonal arrays. However, this can become complicated.

For some exam questions, once the guideline minimum number of rows is known, using elimination of answer options may be appropriate. Options below the guideline minimum can be ruled out, as these are not feasible. The answer options are also likely to include a distractor, a large number typically equal to the total number of pairs, which can also be ruled out. This distractor can also be ruled out. The correct option may be the only remaining option. This should be equal to or greater than the guideline minimum number of rows.

Once the number of rows and columns is determined, a table can be filled in manually or otherwise.

Number of Rows required

A guideline minimum number of rows is straightforward to work out. Use the product of the number of values of the parameter with the most values and the number of values of the parameter with the second highest number of values. For example, in a scenario with three parameters, one having four values, one three values and the third two values, the guideline minimum number of rows is 12 (4 x 3). In another scenario, with four parameters all having three values, 9 (3 x 3) rows are needed.

In all scenarios, determining the actual number of rows can be achieved with a rigorous mathematical approach and use of orthogonal arrays, see *Using Orthogonal Arrays* page 43. This approach is needed for many scenarios with large numbers of parameters and parameter-values. Calculating the number of rows for such a scenario is unlikely to occur in the exam. However, an exam question may refer to the principles involved, see *Revision Exercises - exercise 10* page 70. Most likely, the pairwise questions in the exam will be based on a scenario with a small number of parameters and values.

Number of Columns required

Count the number of parameters. There must be as many columns as parameters. When using the orthogonal array approach, additional columns, if they exist in the selected array, can be dropped/left unused.

Example 1: Guideline minimum number of rows equals the number of tests required

Consider a web application specified to operate with:

Type of customer (2): Standard, With Loyalty Cards
Payment system (2): PayPal, Bank Transfer
Browser (2): Chrome, Safari

Using pairwise testing, how many tests are required to cover all parameter-value pairs?

a) 2
b) 3
c) 4
d) 12

Select ONE option

Answer

There are three parameters each with two values. The number of rows using the guideline method is 4 (2 x 2). Option c) is the correct answer.

There are three parameters, so three columns are required. The table can be completed as below:

Test	Customer	Payment	Browser
1	Standard (S)	PayPal™ (P)	Safari (Sf)
2	Standard (S)	Bank Transfer (BT)	Chrome (C)
3	Loyalty Card (LC)	PayPal™ (P)	Chrome (C)
4	Loyalty Card (LC)	Bank Transfer (BT)	Safari (Sf)

Four tests cover all parameter-value pairs:

Test 1 S/P, S/Sf, P/Sf
Test 2 S/BT, S/C, BT/C
Test 3 LC/P, LC/C, P/C
Test 4 LC/BT, LC/Sf, BT/Sf

Here the guideline minimum number of rows is the same as the actual number of rows required. For this scenario, it is straightforward to manually work out the answer as above. Alternatively, using the elimination approach, answer options a) and b) can be ruled out as they are less than the guideline minimum. Option d) is a distractor and can be ruled out as it is the total number of pairs of parameter-values.

Example 2: ISTQB Sample Exam Question #15

'A company offering house insurance policies has several policy options. They depend on the following factors:

Building type: house, semi-detached, apartment building, cottage

Material: wood, concrete, brick, mixed

Location: city, suburb, countryside, wilderness

You are testing the system and using the pairwise technique for creating test cases.

Using the pairwise technique, how many test cases are required to achieve coverage?

a) 16

b) 12

c) 48

d) 4

Select ONE option'

Answer

There are three parameters, each with four values. Selecting two parameters with the highest number of values means any two of the three parameters could be considered. Using the guideline method, the minimum number of rows 16 (4 x 4). This is one of the occasions when the guideline minimum number equals the actual number of rows required to cover all the parameter-value pairs. But if you are not sure you know this to be true, look at the other answer options. Options b) and d) can be discarded. Option c) can be discarded as it is the total number of pairs of parameter-values.

a) is the correct answer.

Example 3: ISTQB Sample Exam Question #16

'Consider a multi-language web application that shall:

- support three different languages: English, French and Japanese

- run on three different browsers: IE8, IE7, Firefox 11

- run on three different operating systems: Windows XP, Windows Vista, Windows7

You have been asked to test the correct behavior of this application for all the possible combinations of languages, browsers and operating systems.

Due to the restricted amount of time you decide to apply the pairwise testing technique for creating test cases.

Using the pairwise technique, what is the MINIMUM number of test cases needed to achieve a full 2-wise coverage?

a) 3

b) 6

c) 9

d) 27

Select ONE option'

Answer
There are three parameters, each with three values. This makes the minimum number of rows 9 (3 x 3). This is one of the few occasions when the guideline minimum number equals the actual number of rows required to cover all the parameter-value pairs. But if you are not sure you know this to be true, look at the other answer options. Options a) and b) can be discarded as they are below the minimum number of rows required. Option d) 27 can be discarded it is the number of tests required for covering all pairs being tested by themselves, pairwise testing would not provide any benefit if this number of tests were required.

c) is the correct answer.

When the Guideline Minimum Number of Rows is not sufficient

You should be aware of the possibility that in many scenarios the guideline minimum number of rows may not indicate the actual minimum number of test cases required for 100% coverage.

BEWARE of a scenario with four parameters each with 2 values. Using the guideline minimum number of rows suggests 4 (2 x 2) rows. However, 6 rows are needed. There are 24 (4 x 3 x 2 x 1) pairs to test. For scenarios with 4 to 7 parameters, each with 2 values, the best fit orthogonal array has 8 rows, this is then reduced to between 6 and 8 as appropriate, depending on the actual number of parameters, see example 4 on the next page.

BEWARE of a scenario with 5 parameters, one has 2 values, the remaining 4 have 3 values. Using the guideline minimum number of rows would suggest 9 (3 x 3) rows. However, this is not adequate.

BEWARE of a scenario with 5 or more parameters with 3 values. Using the guideline minimum number of rows would suggest 9 (3 x 3) rows. However, this is not adequate.

There are other combinations of parameters and parameter-values where the guideline minimum number of rows does not equal the actual number of tests required for minimum coverage of all parameter-value pairs. Some of these are shown in the Taguchi Designs table, *Appendix B.* For a worked example, with five parameters, four with three parameter values, one with two parameter values, see *Appendix B: Using Orthogonal Arrays.*

Example 4: Minimum number of rows does not equal the number of tests required

Consider a web application: specified to operate with:

Type of customer (2): Standard, with Loyalty card
Payment system (2): PayPal, Bank Transfer
Browser (2): Chrome, Safari
Currency (2): USD, GBP

Using pairwise testing, how many tests are required to cover all parameter-value pairs?

a) 2
b) 3
c) 6
d) 24

Select ONE option

Answer

The number of rows using the approximation method described above is 4 (2 x 2). There are four parameters, so three columns are required. The table can be manually completed as shown.

Test Case	Customer	Payment	Browser	Currency
1	Standard (S)	PayPal (P)	Safari (Sf)	USD
2	Standard (S)	Bank Transfer (BT)	Chrome (C)	GBP
3	Loyalty Card (LC)	PayPal (P)	Chrome (C)	USD
4	Loyalty Card (LC)	Bank Transfer (BT)	Safari (Sf)	GBP

Test 1 S/P, S/Sf, S/USD, P/Sf, P/USD, Sf/USD
Test 2 S/BT, S/C, S/GBP, BT/C, BT/GBP, C/GBP
Test 3 LC/P, LC/C, LC/USD, P/C, C/USD (where P/USD is a duplicate)
Test 4 LC/BT, LC/Sf, LC/GBP, BT/Sf, Sf/GBP (where BT/GBP is a duplicate)

Tests are missing for the pairs P/GBP and BT/USD in the above test cases. The actual number of tests required in this scenario is greater than the guideline minimum. In a scenario with a small number of parameters and parameter-values, it is possible to work out the extra rows required manually, the table can be amended as follows. (A tilde '~' indicates either type of Customer or Browser).

Test Case	Customer	Payment	Browser	Currency
1	Standard (S)	PayPal (P)	Safari (Sf)	USD
2	Standard (S)	Bank Transfer (BT)	Chrome (C)	GBP
3	Loyalty Card (LC)	PayPal (P)	Chrome (C)	USD
4	Loyalty Card (LC)	Bank Transfer (BT)	Safari (Sf)	GBP
5	~	PayPal	~	GBP
6	~	Bank Transfer	~	USD

Option c) is the correct answer. Six test cases are required to cover the 24 parameter-value pairs.

Using elimination, the guideline minimum means answer options a) and b) can be ruled out. d) is the distractor.

Using Orthogonal Arrays for Pairwise Testing

The guideline minimum method above has significant limitations. These limitations do not occur when using the orthogonal array method.

Orthogonal arrays are pre-defined mathematical tables. They provide a systematic way to determine the actual number of rows (test cases) required to test all parameter-value pairs in all scenarios. Working with orthogonal arrays can take time and relies on having an orthogonal array design. As previously mentioned, this technique is particularly useful for scenarios with large numbers of parameters and parameter-value pairs where the guideline minimum number of rows is insufficient for the actual number of rows required to test all parameter-value pairs, see *Appendix B: Using Orthogonal Arrays.*

Although orthogonal arrays are no longer mentioned in the Syllabus 2019, having some knowledge of their use in pairwise testing helps with understanding pairwise testing, producing pairwise test tables and knowing how many test cases are required. For a summary of the steps involved, see *Revision Exercises - exercise 10.* The exam questions are not likely to require more than an overview of the use of orthogonal arrays.

Select an Orthogonal Array

Creating an orthogonal array from scratch is beyond the scope of what is required here. Use a table, such as the one in *Appendix B: Using Orthogonal Arrays,* to establish which array is required.

Columns required in an Orthogonal Array

Count the number of parameters. In the array selected, there must be at least as many columns as parameters. Additional columns, if they exist in the orthogonal array selected, can be dropped or left unused.

Numbers within columns in an Orthogonal Array

Count the number of parameter-values for each parameter. A column must have at least as many numbers within it as the parameter being mapped to the column has values. For example, if the parameter is 'brand' with three possible brand values, the column must contain at least three numbers such as 0, 1, 2 or 1, 2, 3. When there are fewer values than the numbers available in a particular column, during the mapping, a higher number which is not required can be replaced by a tilde '~'.

Number of rows required in an Orthogonal Array

Select an orthogonal array entry from the table in *Appendix B: Using Orthogonal Arrays*, or another reliable source. The table indicates the number of rows for different numbers of parameters and parameter-value pairs. These tables are often called Taguchi Designs or Taguchi Tables. Arrays for larger numbers of parameters and parameter-values as well as more combinations of parameters with different numbers of parameter-values to those included in the table in *Appendix B* are available from various sources, see *References* Section.

Map parameter values onto the array

Assign a parameter to each column. Select one column at a time and map the value for that parameter on to the numbers. Do this by replacing each occurrence of 1 with the first value of that parameter and each occurrence of 2 with the second value of that parameter. Continue for all additional values. If the column has higher numbers than required, replace these with tilde '~'.

Example 5: Using an Orthogonal Array

With the same scenario as in example 4, consider a web application having:

Type of customer: Standard (1), with Loyalty card (2)
Payment system: PayPal (1), Bank transfer (2)
Browser: Chrome (1), Safari (2)
Currency: USD (1), GBP (2)

Using pairwise testing, how many tests are required to cover all parameter-value pairs?

a) 2
b) 3
c) 6
d) 24

Select ONE option

Answer

As shown in example 4, using the guideline minimum number of rows 4 (2 x 2), does not provide enough rows. The correct answer can be obtained using an orthogonal array selected from the table Taguchi Designs, *Appendix B*. The array required is L8 2^7, an array with 8 rows, 2 values for parameters and 7 columns.

	1	**2**	**3**	**4**	**5**	**6**	**7**
1	1	1	1	1	1	1	1
2	1	1	1	2	2	2	2
3	1	2	2	1	1	2	2
4	1	2	2	2	2	1	1
5	2	1	2	1	2	1	2
6	2	1	2	2	1	2	1
7	2	2	1	1	2	2	1
8	2	2	1	2	1	1	2

With four parameters, columns 5, 6 and 7 can be dropped. Mapping the array results in:

Test Case	Customer	Payment	Browser	Currency
1	Standard	PayPal	Chrome	USD
2	Standard	PayPal	Chrome	GBP
3	Standard	Bank Transfer	Safari	USD
4	Standard	Bank Transfer	Safari	GBP
5	Loyalty Card	PayPal	Safari	USD
6	Loyalty Card	PayPal	Safari	GBP
7	Loyalty Card	Bank Transfer	Chrome	USD
8	Loyalty Card	Bank Transfer	Chrome	GBP

The eight rows (test cases) above guarantee all pairs are tested.

1 Standard/PayPal, Standard/Chrome, Standard/USD, PayPal/Chrome, PayPal/USD, Chrome/USD
2 **Standard/PayPal**, **Standard/Chrome**, Standard/GBP, **PayPal/Chrome**, **PayPal/GBP**, Chrome/GBP
3 Standard/Bank Transfer, Standard/Safari, **Standard/USD**, Bank Transfer/Safari, Bank Transfer/USD, Safari/USD
4 **Standard/Bank Transfer**, **Standard/Safari**, **Standard/GBP**, **Bank Transfer/Safari**, Bank Transfer/GBP, **Safari/GBP**
5 Loyalty Card/PayPal, Loyalty Card/Safari, Loyalty Card/USD, PayPal/Safari, **PayPal/USD**, **Safari/USD**
6 **Loyalty Card/PayPal, Loyalty Card/Safari**, Loyalty Card/GBP, **PayPal/Safari**, PayPal/GBP**,** Safari/GBP
7 Loyalty Card/Bank Transfer, Loyalty Card/Chrome, **Loyalty Card/USD**, Bank Transfer/Chrome, **Bank Transfer/USD**
8 **Loyalty Card/Bank Transfer, Loyalty Card/Chrome**, **Loyalty Card/GBP**, **Bank Transfer/Chrome**, **Bank Transfer/GBP**

If the selected array has duplicate parameter-value pairs, as is the case here, on inspection it is possible to reduce the rows. The entries shown in **bold** above are not required as the combinations they produce occur elsewhere. Deleting these leaves 24 pairs as below.

1 Standard/PayPal, Standard/Chrome, Standard/USD, PayPal/Chrome, PayPal/USD, Chrome/USD
2 Standard/GBP, Chrome/GBP
3 Standard/Bank Transfer, Standard/Safari, Bank Transfer/Safari, Bank Transfer/USD, Safari/USD
4 Bank Transfer/GBP
5 Loyalty Card/PayPal, Loyalty Card/Safari, Loyalty Card/USD, PayPal/Safari
6 Loyalty Card/GBP, PayPal/GBP, Safari/GBP
7 Loyalty Card/Bank Transfer, Loyalty Card/Chrome, Bank Transfer/Chrome

The table now becomes:

Test Case	Customer	Payment	Browser	Currency
1	Standard	PayPal	Chrome	USD
2	Standard	~	Chrome	GBP
3	Standard	Bank Transfer	Safari	USD
4	~	Bank Transfer	~	GBP
5	Loyalty Card	PayPal	Safari	USD
6	Loyalty Card	PayPal	Safari	GBP
7	Loyalty Card	Bank Transfer	Chrome	~
8	~	~	~	~

Row 2 and row 4 can be merged by resetting row 2 payment to Bank Transfer*.

The final table is:

Test Case	Customer	Payment	Browser	Currency
1	Standard	PayPal	Chrome	USD
2	Standard	Bank Transfer*	Chrome	GBP
3	Standard	Bank Transfer	Safari	USD
4				
5	Loyalty Card	PayPal	Safari	USD
6	Loyalty Card	PayPal	Safari	GBP
7	Loyalty Card	Bank Transfer	Chrome	~
8				

Twenty-four pairs can be tested with six remaining test cases which makes c) the correct answer.

Alternatively, using the elimination method, options a) and b) can be discarded as they are below the guideline minimum number 4 (2 x 2). Option d) is a distractor, this is the total number of pairs. This leaves option c) as the correct answer.

USER STORIES AND USE CASES

User stories and use cases contain some similar elements. Both should be written from the user's perspective. However, a user story is not the same as a use case, they serve different purposes.

User Stories

A user story focuses on what the user needs. This allows for further discussion on how added value can be included in the system. User story is included in the Syllabus, chapter 5 *Reviews*. In Agile projects, requirements usually take the form of user stories. A 'user story model' is the set of all user stories which reflects the user's needs.

The ISTQB Glossary definition of user story is, *'a user or business requirement consisting of one sentence expressed in the everyday or business language which is capturing the functionality a user needs, the reason behind it, any non-functional criteria, and also including acceptance criteria.'* 'User story' is not shown as a keyword for the Test Analyst in either the Syllabus or the Glossary v3.3, but is included in both and is an essential term to know and understand.

The ISO 26515 definition of 'User Story' is, *'a simple narrative illustrating a user requirement from the perspective of a persona.'*

User stories represent small units of demonstrable functionality. A user story often starts in the same way as a use case, describing a goal for a particular user. Typically, the reason for achieving the goal is specified. The accepted language of the user and business is used. A user story may not be documented to the same level of detail as a use case is.

Using the ISTQB Glossary definition above for a user story being one sentence, the user or business requirement typically follows the format:

As an [actor] I want [some goal] so that [some reason].

This sentence must be clear and distinct with testable acceptance criteria. The goal must be an achievement aim and not an actor's task list. The actor can be:

Principle actor:	has user goals fulfilled by using the system.
Supporting actor:	provides a service to the system, for example the billing fulfilment component of an online ordering application.
Offstage actor:	has an interest in the behaviour of the object under test, such as a regulatory body auditing the application.

Checklists can be built from the acceptance criteria for a user story. A checklist for the user story itself is given in the Syllabus, page 47.

Examples of user stories:
As a new user to the website, I want to register so that I can browse and buy listed products.

As a Marketing Manager, I want to, for specified periods, apply free delivery to online orders for goods listed on our website where the order is for more than a specified amount so that I can run promotions.

As a Regulatory Compliance Officer, I want reports on truck drivers' hours so that I can monitor compliance with regulations on maximum hours worked.

More detailed example:
User Story name: Analytics reports on sales   User Story ID/target sprint:
Priority: High
Story: As a Sales Manager I want to run analytics reports on sales data
so that I can keep track of future expected monthly income.

Action	**Acceptance Criteria**
User logs in	Credentials checked; login confirmed
System displays options	User selects sales report
User enters time period	Report generated
User requests printout	Report printed
User elects to save report	Report saved in online repository

Use Cases

A use case focuses on what the component or system should deliver. A use case is a user transaction that can traverse multiple areas of functionality. Compared to a user story, a use case has a more detailed specification of a requirement. A 'use case model' is the set of all use cases which reflect the component's or system's functionality.

A definition of 'use case' is not included in the Glossary. 'Use case testing' is included in the Syllabus chapter 3 *Test Techniques* and in the Glossary, *'A black-box test technique in which test cases are designed to exercise use case behaviors'*. A checklist for use cases is included in the Syllabus chapter 5 *Reviews.*

The ISO 26515 definition of 'Use Case' is, *'A description of behavioural requirements of a system and its interaction with a user. A use case describes the users' goal and the requirements including the sequence of interactions between users and the system'.*

A use case has a single main path, optionally with alternative paths that later return to the main path or terminate the use case early. The use case thus covers the related success and failure outcomes in achieving the goal.

Use cases can be a paragraph covering the details. But a more formal layout is likely to provide additional benefit. An example of a layout is below. In an exam situation, with time and space constraints, a question on use case may not include all elements of this layout.

USE CASE: Name
Identifier: Unique reference
Purpose or Scope: The goal
Actor(s): Entity or entities that use the system and show a behaviour
Precondition(s): What must be true at the start
Post-condition(s): What must be true on successful completion
Special requirements: Related non-functional requirements
Technology and data variations: Varying I/O methods and data formats
Priority:
Additional Considerations:
Main success scenario/flow with alternate paths where specified:

When writing the scenario/flow, focus on the actor's intentions and the system's responsibilities. There is no need to include the user interface layout. Consider what the system must do, not on the detail of how it does it. For example:

Good –	System records order
Bad –	System writes order to database
Poor –	System generates mySQL INSERT statement for order

The main success scenario/flow can be written in either one or two columns. With one column, steps are listed sequentially in the order they occur. Using two columns emphasizes the actor and the component or system interaction.

Example of a Use Case
USE CASE: Checking out a basket of goods
Use case ID: UC-2828
Purpose: Confirm details (delivery address, delivery option and payment details) to complete order
Actors: Registered user wishing to purchase goods
Preconditions: Logged-in user with an existing account, items in basket
Post-condition: User given Tracking ID
Special requirements: Order and user Tracking ID must be recorded in the system's log
Related non-functional requirements: Indicator for user must appear when system is processing
Technology and data variations: Keyboard alternatives must be available for mouse actions
Priority: High
Additional considerations: Tracking ID should have details of order, delivery address, payment made and cost (goods plus delivery charge)

(continued on next page)

Flow using one column:

1. User confirms order is complete
2. System presents user with order details and delivery address
3. User confirms displayed delivery address should be used (alternate path: user elects to use different delivery address, system validates and records)
4. System displays relevant account details for payment method
5. User confirms displayed payment method should be used (alternate path: user elects to different payment method, system validates and records, use case continues)
6. System displays delivery options (alternate path: user abandons order)
7. User selects delivery option (alternate path: user abandons order, use case ends)
8. System requests billing system to charge user for order and delivery option
9. System confirms charge has been made, records and provides the user with a Tracking ID

Flow using two columns:

User	**System**
1. Confirms order complete	2. Displays order details and delivery address
3. Confirms displayed delivery address should be used (E1)	4. Displays relevant account details for payment method
5. Confirms displayed payment method should be used (E2)	6. Displays delivery options and costs
7. Selects delivery option (E3)	8. Requests billing system to charge user for order and delivery option
	9. Confirms charge made. Records and provides Tracking ID

Exceptions:

E1: User elects different delivery address. System validates and records. Use case continues
E2: User elects different payment method. System validates and records. Use case continues
E3: User abandons order, for example, delivery times or costs not acceptable. Use case ends

The two test cases, derived from this use case, provide minimum test coverage:

Test case 1: 1, 2, 3, 4, 5, 6, 7, 8, 9 (Main path)
Test case 2: 1, 2, 3, (change delivery address), 4, 5, (change payment), 6, 7, (abandon)

As exceptions E1 and E2 continue the use case, they can be combined in one test case. E3 can be added. If E1 or E2 were to have an option to terminate the use case, thus making it impossible to reach other exceptions in one test case, additional test cases would be required.

Although, in this scenario, only two test cases are required for 100% minimum use case test coverage, in practice it may be advisable to run an additional test where the changes occur and the order is not abandoned. This would allow for the accuracy of information on the Tracking ID to be checked for a changed delivery address or payment method. Designing and executing more test cases than the number suggested by the model used is covered in Chapter *Test Coverage*, where more detail on this example is given.

TEST COVERAGE

Measuring Test Coverage

Test coverage is a measure of the amount of testing as determined or exercised by a set of test cases. The set of test cases, which can be referred to as a test suite or test model, is generally based on a specific test technique, for example decision table, state transition diagram or other. Test coverage can be used as a metric for both test design and test execution activities.

The Glossary specifies test coverage is expressed as a percentage. This can be calculated as follows:

$$\text{Test Coverage} = \frac{\text{Test cases determined or exercised}}{\text{Total possible feasible, non-redundant test cases}} \times 100\%$$

Details for establishing the number of test cases determined or exercised and the total possible number of test cases are included in the Syllabus with the relevant test technique description. These are also listed in the table in *Revision Exercises Answers, exercise 6.* This table should be understood and learned. The exam includes questions on test coverage.

A 100% minimum test coverage indicates all tests relevant to the technique being used have been included. Acceptance criteria for a particular project may specify a lower percentage.

Test coverage measurement typically does not focus test resources on where the greatest use of the application occurs or the most frequently used conditions or combinations of conditions. However, test cases could be subdivided and grouped into specific usage areas. (Risk test coverage is determined by assessment of the impact and likelihood of a defect occurring, not from the test technique model).

When More Test Cases are Required

Additional tests to those suggested by the test model

From the Syllabus '*Completely fulfilling the coverage criteria does not mean that the entire set of tests is complete, but rather that the model no longer suggests any additional tests to increase coverage based on that technique*'.

It is important to consider if the test model being used should be supplemented with additional test cases beyond those for 100% minimum coverage. Additional test cases may be repeated tests or tests from another technique.

The use case example in Chapter *User Stories and Use Cases* for checking out a basket of goods requires two test cases for 100% minimum test coverage. Test case 1 is for the main path and ends with a Tracking ID. Test case 2 covers the 3 exceptions (change of delivery address, change of payment information and when presented with the delivery option, abandon the order). No order is placed and no Tracking ID is issued. To confirm the Tracking ID reflects change of delivery address and payment method, an additional test case where the order is not abandoned is required.

Practice Exam One, question #9 is a scenario where boundary analysis is being used. One of the partitions spans zero. This is not tested as part of 100% minimum test coverage based on boundary analysis as it is not on a boundary. This is a scenario where it would be good practice to add a test to ensure zero is handled correctly.

Repeating tests

A Test Analyst looking to optimize software quality should be aware of the possibility that repeated use of the same test with the same software in the same environment could result in different outcomes. With a defined set of inputs which does not include random data or random manipulation, the application should produce the same outcome irrespective of how many times it is run. This is a key requirement for high-quality deterministic software. It is also possible, that running the same test repeatedly over time in the same environment, results in degradation of the response time or another resource. 'Repeatability' should not be confused with the ISTQB term 'reusability' which is defined as, '*the degree to which a work product can be used in more than one system, or in building other work products.*' Repeating tests should also not be confused with regression testing which is conducted when there is a change to the system and defects may have been introduced.

Different outcomes can occur due to a variety of reasons. These include variables not correctly initialised, repeated use of temporary areas or files not intended for reuse, undetected memory leaks, numerical inaccuracies, incorrect pointers, buffer overflow or underflow and other problems. Also, the system's substantive behaviour may be dependent on the sequence or timing of uncontrollable events, multithreading conflicts or cyclic interaction. For example, software controlling a complex set of traffic signals may be affected by such issues. The risk of such failures increases when multiple entities access or modify shared resources in a system. However, this is not necessarily the same as load testing, executing a single test case a number of times could result in failure over time.

Applications, particularly those that have been in use over a long period, may have inherent problems with design flows and numerical inaccuracies when used repeatedly. Complex applications are likely to be at higher risk of these types of defects, particularly when there is a monolithic code base. Although these problems could be viewed as the Technical Test Analyst's responsibilities, failures may occur within any of the areas designated as part of the Test Analyst's responsibilities. It is essential functional correctness, other quality characteristics and sub-characteristics are achieved consistently.

Examples: Scenarios where repeating a test case results in a different outcome
A user orders items online, completes the purchase and logs out. The order is correctly dispatched and billed. The user returns to place a repeat order with the same items but is not able to complete the purchase as the application indicates a pending order. The indicator was not reset at the end of the previous session.

An application processes a large data set and in doing so uses temporary work areas for interim sorting and calculations. One of these areas is not cleared. A repeat of the test case run with the same input data results in sorting and calculations in this area being additive to existing data. When the outcome is checked against the test oracle, the repeat of the test is marked as 'Fail'.

Test Analyst Actions

Avoid complacency in assuming a test will always result in the same outcome. The Test Analyst should always review the test model to ensure a full set of appropriate test cases are considered.

Repeat testing is important if the potential of a particular test having a different outcome could result in a significant adverse impact for the individual or business relying on the application. However, testing cannot continue indefinitely. There are likely to be commercial factors, such as costs or deadlines to be met. The amount of repeat testing that can be conducted will be limited. The Test Analyst, with the Project Manager and other stakeholders, should assess the potential impact and the likelihood of such problems. A decision can then be taken on the amount of repeat testing, if any, that should be conducted and this can be added to the test exit criteria.

The Test Analyst should use best practices throughout, address non-determinism in test planning as appropriate. Emphasis should put on component and integration testing where this can be done. Finding non-determinism at a later stage is typically more difficult. Testing components for a car assembly line for integrity is more likely to result in a car without defects.

When a defect occurs on a repeated test case, the Test Analyst should scrutinize logs to check for timing or other anomalies that may not have been present on the first execution of the test case.

The Test Analyst should, as far as possible, make sure it is understood why the repeat test was unsuccessful to be able to rule out the possibility of this being an isolated result.

Keep in mind the principle of '*Changing Anything Changes Everything*'. Executing a test case in a specific environment could in itself be a change, not obvious at the outset but affecting subsequent use.

MEASURING USABILITY

The Advanced Test Analyst should have some understanding of usability metrics. From the Syllabus, '*Usability testing evaluates the ease by which users can use or learn to use the system to reach a specified goal in a specific context*'. Usability testing is directed at measuring effectiveness, efficiency and satisfaction.

Two types of usability evaluation are identified in the ISTQB Foundation Syllabus for Usability Testing Specialist (2018). Formative (or exploratory) evaluation is conducted to understand usability issues and can be used to guide the design by identifying usability design problems. Summative evaluation is conducted to quantitatively measure the usability of a component or software product. It focuses on obtaining measurements for the effectiveness, efficiency or satisfaction of a software product. Summative usability evaluation can be used to evaluate a design based on usability requirements so that the design's acceptability can be established from the users' point of view.

Having usability measurements means applications can be evaluated and comparisons made between applications or versions of applications. Targets and verifiable goals can be set for the user experience. The metrics may highlight good and less good aspects of the application.

Using Documents that Specify Usability Requirements

Usability can be measured by recording the extent to which the component or system meets detailed documented usability requirements. These requirements must be:

Clear:	Understandable and unambiguous
Consistent:	Do not contradict or negate the other requirements
Complete:	All that is needed is fully stated

Reporting the percentage of requirements met when there is no weighting factor against the requirement is a blunt technique of assessing usability as some requirements will be more important than others. The documented usability requirements can be split into lists based on weighting factors and percentages for each list can be reported.

Example 1: User interface requirements that could be included in a usability document

1. Company logo must appear in the upper right corner of each relevant page.
   It must meet the company logo regulations for size, orientation and colour.
   Clicking on the logo must cause a return to the home page
2. Button spacing must be: 12-24 pixels for a large button, 24-36 pixels for a medium button, 36-48 pixels for a small button
3. An indicator must appear when the system is processing
4. Keyboard alternatives must be available for mouse actions

Usability Terms

Knowing and understanding the following definitions is essential for the methods that follow.

Usability Term	Definition
Effectiveness	Extent to which correct and complete goals are achieved (ISTQB Glossary)
Efficiency	Degree to which resources are expended in relation to the results achieved (ISTQB Glossary)
Satisfaction*	Capability of the test object to satisfy users in a specified context of use (ISO 25010)

* See Measuring Satisfaction later for full ISO 2510 definition.

The term 'task' is used in this chapter for a test case or a test suite as appropriate.

Measuring Effectiveness

Effectiveness - Number of Errors

The number of errors users make when attempting to complete a task can be recorded. Errors may be unintended actions, slips, mistakes or omissions. A short description, severity rating and classification of each error under the respective category can be collected. The number of errors, (total overall or for a particular classification or a particular severity), per user is calculated and used for comparisons. The process can provide valuable information on where changes could be made to make the system easier to use. However, the process may be time-consuming.

Example 2: Calculation of Effectiveness based on number of errors

Four users perform the same task using the same system. The task has a defined goal. Two users complete the task with no unintended actions, slips, mistakes or omissions. One user rotated the screen and the display did not adjust. This was deemed a severe error. The fourth user made three slips navigating the screens, these were deemed low severity errors.

Total number of errors for this task = 4 (1 + 3)
Number of errors per user for this task = 1
Number of high severity errors per user for this task = 1 divided by 4 = 0.25
Number of low severity errors per user for this task = 3 divided by 4 = 0.75

Effectiveness - Completion Rate

Effectiveness can be evaluated from the completion of specified tasks and then presented as a percentage.

$$\text{Effectiveness for completion rate} = \frac{\text{Number of tasks completed successfully}}{\text{Total number of tasks undertaken}} \times 100\%$$

Example 3: Calculation of Effectiveness based on completion rate

Four users perform the same task using the same system. The task has a defined goal. At the end of the test session, 3 users achieve the goal of the task while the fourth user does not.

Number of tasks completed successfully = 3
Total number of tasks undertaken = 4
Inserting these above values into the equation above:

$$\text{Effectiveness for completion rate} = \frac{3}{4} \times 100 = 75\%$$

Example 4: Graph of Effectiveness based on completion rate

Effectiveness can be shown graphically. Users perform the same three tasks using the same system. Each task has a defined goal. The number of users completing each task is recorded. Effectiveness based on completion rate for each task is calculated as in example 3 above.

The result is presented in the graph below:

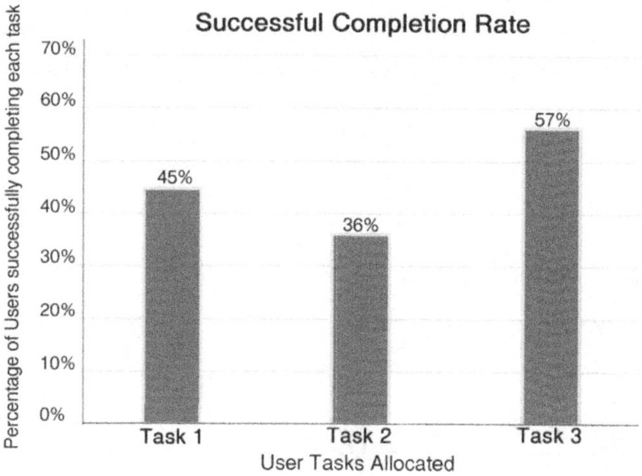

Measuring Efficiency

Efficiency – Task Time

Efficiency is measured in terms of the resources expended. One of the resources is task time, the time a user takes to complete a task (goal) successfully or the time for a user to abandon it.

Task Time = End Time – Start Time

Efficiency - Time-Based

$$\text{Time Based Efficiency} = \frac{\sum_{j=1}^{R}\sum_{i=1}^{N}\frac{n_{ij}}{t_{ij}}}{NR}$$

where

N = total number of tasks
R = number of users

n_{ij} = result of task i by user j; if the user completes the task successfully, then n_{ij} = 1, otherwise n_{ij} = 0

t_{ij} = time spent by user j to complete task i. If the task is not completed successfully, time is measured till the moment the user abandons the task

Example 5: Calculation of Time-based Efficiency

Four users perform the same task using the same system. The task has a defined goal. Three users complete the task successfully, taking 1, 2 and 4 minutes respectively. The fourth user takes 6 minutes and then gives up without completing the task.

Using the above equation:

N = Total number of tasks = 1
R = Number of users = 4

User 1: n_{ij} = 1 and t_{ij} = 1 User 2: n_{ij} = 1 and t_{ij} = 2

User 3: n_{ij} = 1 and t_{ij} = 4 User 4: n_{ij} = 0 and t_{ij} = 6

$$\text{Time Based Efficiency} = \frac{\frac{1}{1}+\frac{1}{2}+\frac{1}{4}+\frac{0}{6}}{1 \times 4} = 0.44 \ \textit{goals/min}$$

Efficiency - Relative Overall

The overall relative efficiency uses the ratio of the time taken by the users who completed the task (goal) successfully in relation to the total time taken by all users.

$$\text{Overall Relative Efficiency} = \frac{\sum_{j=1}^{R}\sum_{i=1}^{N} n_{ij}t_{ij}}{\sum_{j=1}^{R}\sum_{i=1}^{N} t_{ij}} \times 100\%$$

where

N = total number of tasks
R = number of users

nij = result of task i by user j; if the user completes the task successfully, then nij = 1, otherwise nij = 0

tij = time spent by user j to complete the task i. If the task is not completed successfully, the time is measured until the user abandons the task.

Example 6: Calculation of Overall Relative Efficiency

Four users perform the same task using the same system. The task has a defined goal. Three users manage to complete the task successfully, taking 1, 2 and 4 minutes respectively. The fourth user takes 6 minutes and then gives up without completing the task.

Using the equation above:

N = total number of tasks = 1
R = number of users = 4

User 1: nij = 1 and tij = 1

User 2: nij = 1 and tij = 2

User 3: nij = 1 and tij = 4

User 4: nij = 0 and tij = 6

$$\text{Overall Relative Efficiency} = \left(\frac{(1 \times 1) + (1 \times 2) + (1 \times 4) + (0 \times 6)}{1 + 2 + 4 + 6}\right) \times 100 = 54\%$$

Measuring Satisfaction

Understanding the term 'satisfaction' helps with focusing on what testing is required. 'Satisfaction' is the user's response to interaction with the application and includes attitudes towards use of the application. The term 'satisfaction' is not included in the ISTQB Glossary v3.3. Consider the definitions below from ISO 25010 - Chapter 4 Terms and definitions.

Definition - Satisfaction

The degree to which user needs are satisfied when a product or system is used in a specified context of use. There are four sub-characteristics of usefulness, trust, pleasure and comfort.

Four Sub-characteristics of Satisfaction

Usefulness: The degree to which a user is satisfied with their perceived achievement of pragmatic goals, including the results of use and the consequences of use.

Trust: The degree to which a user or other stakeholder has confidence that a product or system will behave as intended.

Pleasure: The degree to which a user obtains pleasure from fulfilling their personal needs. Personal needs can include needs to acquire new knowledge and skills, to communicate personal identity and to provoke pleasant memories.

Comfort: The degree to which the user is satisfied with physical comfort.

Reviews, usability surveys and questionnaires targeted at particular aspects of satisfaction can be used. Percentages can be calculated. These allow for benchmarking against a database of previous usability measurements.

Example 8: Use of SUMI

SUMI provides quantitative measurements of usability, as shown below:

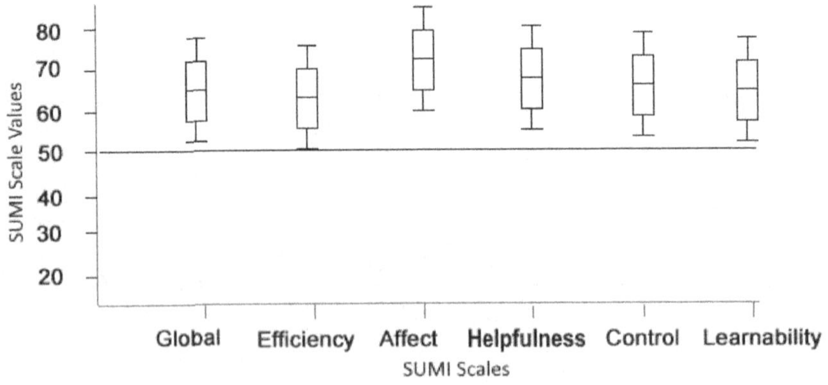

REVISION EXERCISES - QUESTIONS

In this section, you will find ten revision exercises. These exercises are designed to check your knowledge on some specific points. They are intentionally not in the format of the exam questions.

Exercise 1: V-model

In the software development life cycle, the V-model represents a development process that may be considered an extension of the waterfall model. The V-model is included in the ISTQB Foundation Level and is mentioned in the Advanced Test Analyst Syllabus. The Foundation Syllabus underpins the Advanced Test Analyst materials and may be examined.

Fill in the boxes in the V-model diagram below:

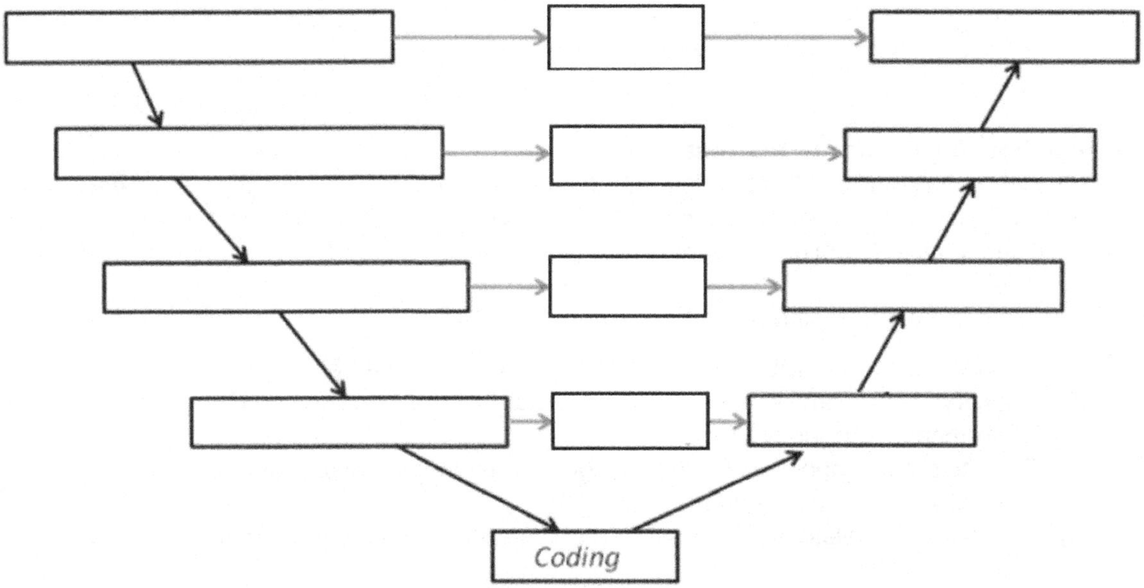

Exercise 2: The Test Process

The test process described in the ISTQB Foundation Level has seven activities. In the Advanced Test Analyst Syllabus, four of these activities, which have particular relevance for the Test Analyst are considered in more depth. In the box below, the activity, 'Monitoring and Control' has been filled in. Revise the test process by filling in each of the six boxes in the test process diagram below with a different activity. The activity's position should be in the appropriate box position in the project timeline. Mark with ATA, the four activities which have particular relevance for the Test Analyst.

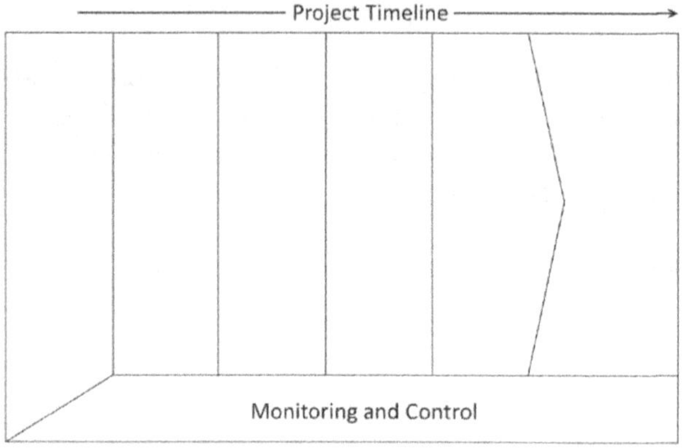

Exercise 3: Responsibilities of the Test Analyst

Which of the following software characteristics and sub-characteristics are specified as a Test Analyst's responsibility or shared responsibility between the Test Analyst and Technical Test Analyst?
For each list, underline the term or terms that are a Test Analyst's responsibility or shared responsibility.

A list may have between none and all its entries underlined.

a) Interoperability, operability, co-existence, portability, time behaviour, security
b) Functional correctness, accessibility, adaptability, analyzability, user interface aesthetics, performance, efficiency
c) Fault-tolerance, appropriateness recognizability, functional appropriateness, user error protection, learnability, maturity
d) Functional completeness, reliability, robustness, resource utilization, replaceability, installability
e) Confidentiality, integrity, authenticity, availability, capacity, recoverability
f) Modifiability, modularity, reusability, accountability, non-repudiation, testability
g) Functional suitability, usability, conformity, sizability

Exercise 4: Risk Assessment

A Test Analyst should contribute to identifying and assessing the potential business domain or user impact for risk items.

Fill in the blanks below with words beginning with the letters indicated:

i) Frequency of use of the a .... f ....
ii) B .... loss
iii) F .... damage
iv) Ecological or social l .... or l ....
v) Civil or criminal l .... s ....
vi) Safety c ....
vii) F ...., loss of l ....
viii) Lack of r .... w .... if people cannot work any more
ix) Visibility of the f ....
x) Visibility of failure leading to negative p .... and potential i .... damage
xi) Loss of c ....

Exercise 5: Test Techniques

Match the test technique to the correct description. Fill in the answer box descriptions with the appropriate letter.

	Test Technique / Testing
1	Decision tables
2	Defect-based
3	Exploratory
4	Boundary Value Analysis
5	Error guessing
6	Pairwise
7	Equivalence partitioning
8	Use case
9	State transition
10	Checklist-based

	Description
a.	Test cases are designed to exercise the combinations of conditions and resulting actions shown
b.	Charters may be designed for specific tasks and objectives. Testing is planned to achieve these criteria
c.	Derives test cases from taxonomies
d.	Group test conditions into partitions that will be processed in the same manner
e.	Uses Test Analyst's experience to guess potential errors
f.	Scenario-based testing that emulates intended use of the component or system
g.	All valid states and transitions are tested
h.	Defines and tests for the boundaries of partitions
i.	Test cases are designed to exercise parameter-value pairs
j.	Uses a high-level generalised list of items or a set of rules or criteria against which a product has to be verified

Answer Box

Test Technique / Testing	Description	Test Technique / Testing	Description
1		6	
2		7	
3		8	
4		9	
5		10	

Exercise 6: Minimum Test Coverage

The Test Analyst needs to be aware of coverage for each test technique. Complete the following tables with a short description of how coverage is evaluated.

Specification-based Techniques / Testing

Test Technique / Testing	Coverage (x100 to express as a percentage of minimum test coverage)
Equivalence Partitioning	
Boundary Value Analysis	
Decision Tables	
State Transition	
Pairwise	
Use Case	

Defect-based Technique

Test Technique / Testing	Coverage (x100 to express as a percentage of minimum test coverage)
Defect Taxonomies	

Experience-based Techniques

Test Technique / Testing	Coverage (x100 to express as a percentage of minimum test coverage)
Error Guessing	
Checklist-Based	
Exploratory	

Exercise 7: The Test Process

The Test Analyst needs a thorough understanding of the test process. The Syllabus gives an example of how the fundamental test process applied to the system test level could align in the sequential V-model. Look at list 1 and put an identifier in the correct order in column 1. Then select a corresponding part of a sentence from list 2, put its identifier in column 2 and if applicable add an identifier from list 3 to make seven complete statements.

Statement	One from List 1	One from List 2	One from List 3 (if appropriate)
1			
2			
3			
4			
5			
6			
7			

List 1

a) System test completion activities occur after
b) System test environment implementation might start during
c) Test monitoring and control continues until
d) System test planning occurs concurrently with
e) System test analysis and design occur concurrently with
f) System test execution begins when
g) System test execution continues until

List 2

i) project planning
ii) the system test exit criteria are met
iii) system design though the bulk of it typically would occur concurrently with
iv) requirements specification, system and architectural (high-level) design specification, and component (low-level) design specification
v) the system test entry criteria are all met (or waived) which
vi) system test execution and closure are complete
vii) the system test exit criteria are met

List 3

y) coding and component test with work on system test implementation activities stretching often until just days before the start of system test execution
z) typically means that at least component testing and often also component integration testing have met their exit criteria or definitions of done

Exercise 8: Glossary Terms

Understanding the keywords is an essential requirement. Other terms should also be understood. Use the following to check your understanding of some terms. This exercise is based on the Glossary v3.3 and updates made to June 2020.

The definition is given, what is the term? Write your answer under each definition.

Glossary List 1

i) The behaviour produced/observed when a component or system is tested.

ii) A type of formal review to identify issues in a work product, which provides measurement to improve the review process and the software development process.

iii) A type of review that follows a defined process with a formally documented output.

iv) The degree to which test conditions can be established for a component or system and tests can be performed to determine whether those test conditions have been met.

v) The degree to which a component or system can function correctly in the presence of invalid inputs or stressful environmental conditions.

Glossary List 2

vi) A scripting technique in which test scripts contain high-level keywords and supporting files that contain low-level scripts that implement those keywords.

vii) An iterative incremental framework for managing projects.

viii) An independent examination of a work product or process performed by a third party to assess whether it complies with specifications, standards, contractual agreements or other criteria.

ix) Extent to which correct and complete goals are achieved.

x) A part of a series of web accessibility guidelines published by the Web Accessibility Initiative (WAI) of the World Wide Web Consortium (W3C), the main international standards organization of the internet.

Glossary List 3

xi) The degree to which resources are expended in relation to results achieved.

xii) The set of conditions for officially starting a defined task.

xiii) The observable predicted behavior of a test item under specified conditions based on its test basis.

xiv) An event in which a component or system does not perform a required function within specified limits.

xv) A type of change-related testing to detect whether defects have been introduced or uncovered in unchanged areas of the software.

Glossary List 4

xvi) A measurement scale and the method used for measurement.

xvii) A test suite that covers the main functionality of a component or system to determine whether it works properly before planned testing begins.

xviii) An instance of the test process against a single identifiable version of the test object.

xix) A source to determine expected results to compare with the actual result of the software under test.

xx) The degree of impact that a defect has on the development or operation of a component or system.

Glossary List 5

xxi) The activity to select data from existing databases or create, generate, manipulate data for testing.

xxii) The degree to which a component or system protects users against making errors.

xxiii) A test case with abstract preconditions, input data, expected results, post-conditions and actions (where applicable).

xxiv) Documentation of the goal or objective for a test session.

xxv) Data needed for test execution.

Exercise 9: Test Design

Test cases can be classified as high-level or low-level. The Test Analyst should determine which is the most appropriate for a given situation. Which of the following statements apply to high-level test cases and which to low-level test cases?

Fill in column one of the tables below and the two asterisked gaps with either 'high-level' or 'low-level'

Test Types box 1

Test Cases	Statement
	Can be referred to as concrete test cases
	Provide all the specific information and procedures needed for the tester to execute the test case (including any data requirements) and verify the results
	Tend to limit tester ingenuity (limit latitude) during execution
	Best when documentation is clearly defined
	May result in loss of reproducibility

Test Types box 2

Test Cases	Statement
	Best used when the tester is experienced with both testing and the product (experienced staff)
	Also referred to as logical test cases
	Formal documentation is not required (e.g. no audits)
	May require a significant amount of maintenance
	May be defined early in the requirements process when requirements are not yet well-defined

Test Types box 3

Test Cases	Statement
	Can be used to develop ___________* test cases.
	Best when external verification of the tests (such as audits) is required
	Latitude (ingenuity) to vary data and actual steps in the business process
	May provide better coverage than ___________* test cases because they will vary each time they are executed.
	Tests are easily reproducible

Exercise 10: Pairwise Testing

You have decided to use pairwise testing with orthogonal arrays. The following steps are all part of the process to be followed. What is the correct order of these steps that you should follow to complete the task?

A. Construct the test cases
B. Determine the number of values for each parameter
C. Map onto the orthogonal array
D. Identify and determine the number of parameters
E. Select an appropriate orthogonal array

Fill in the table below:

Step 1	Step 2	Step 3	Step 4	Step 5

REVISION EXERCISES - ANSWERS

Exercise 1: V-model

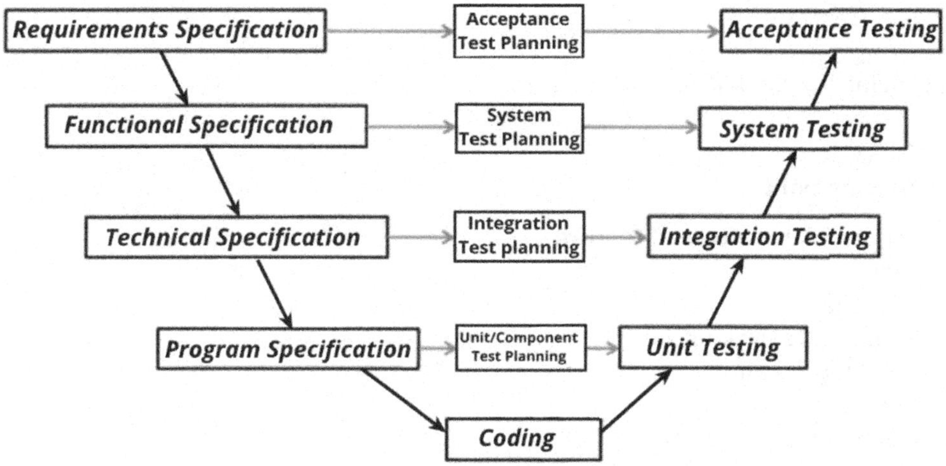

Exercise 2: The Test Process

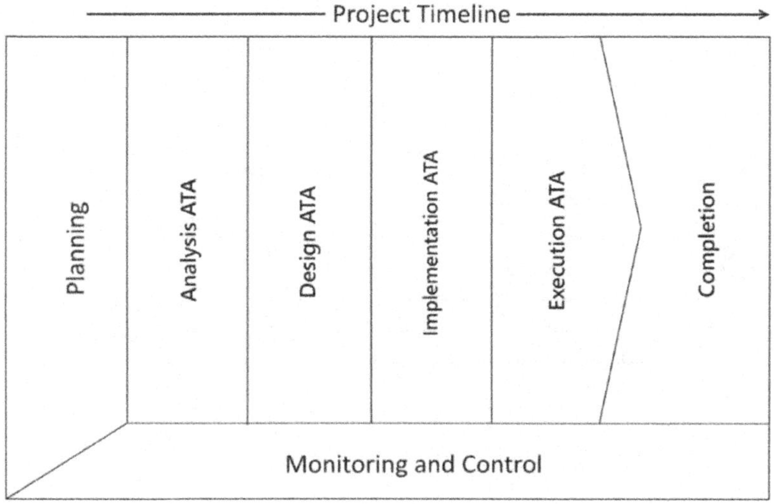

Exercise 3: Responsibilities of the Test Analyst

a) Interoperability, operability, portability
b) Functional correctness, accessibility, adaptability, user interface aesthetics
c) Appropriateness recognizability, functional appropriateness, user error protection, learnability
d) Functional completeness, replaceability, installability
e) None
f) None
g) Functional suitability, usability

Exercise 4: Risk Assessment

i) Frequency of use of the **affected feature**
ii) **Business** loss
iii) **Financial** damage
iv) Ecological or social **losses or liability**
v) Civil or criminal **legal sanctions**
vi) Safety **concerns**
vii) **Fines,** loss of **license**
viii) Lack of **reasonable workarounds** if people cannot work any more
ix) Visibility of the **feature**
x) Visibility of failure leading to negative **publicit**y and potential **image** damage
xi) Loss of **customers**

Exercise 5: Test Techniques / Testing

Test Technique/ Testing	Description	Test Technique/ Testing	Description
1	**a**	6	**i**
2	**c**	7	**d**
3	**b**	8	**f**
4	**h**	9	**g**
5	**e**	10	**j**

Exercise 6: Minimum Test Coverage

Test Technique	**Coverage** (x100 to express as a percentage of minimum test coverage)
Equivalence Partitioning	The number of partitions for which a value has been tested divided by the number of partitions that have been identified. Using multiple values for a single partition does not increase the coverage percentage.
Boundary Value Analysis	The number of boundary conditions tested divided by the number of identified boundary conditions (either using the two-value or three-value technique).
Decision Tables	**Covering all condition outcomes**: the number of columns where tests have been conducted divided by the total number of columns. (Note: From the Syllabus, the total number of columns is *'2 to the power of the number of conditions',* this is only true when all conditions are limited to having two values each). **Covering all actions:** sufficient decision rules are applied to generate all possible expected actions. **Covering all non-redundant and feasible decision rules**: columns in a fully collapsed decision table are covered. A collapsed table generates fewer tests than a full table. **Covering Individual outcomes**: the number of columns where tests have been conducted divided by the total number of columns. (Note: From the Syllabus, the total number of columns is *'the number of conditions plus 1',* this is only true when all conditions are limited to having two values each).
State Transition Testing	100% minimum coverage is to have visited every state and traversed every transition at least once. **n-switch coverage:** the number of switches covered of length (n+1) divided by the total number of switches of that length. **Round-trip coverage**: irrespective of the loop size, the number of loops traversed divided by the total number of all loops from any state back to the same state.
Pairwise	The number of parameter-value pairs tested once against a parameter-value pair of another parameter divided the number of all parameter-value pairs tested once against **each** parameter-value pair of **every** other parameter that can be tested. This is not the number of tests derived from a pairwise table, where one test covers multiple pairs.
Use case	Tests needed include one test for the basic behaviour (main path) plus sufficient additional test cases to cover each alternate and error handling behaviour. Coverage is the number of these tests conducted divided by the total number of tests needed.

Defect-based Technique

Test Technique	**Coverage** (x100 to express as a percentage of minimum test coverage)
Defect taxonomies	Coverage items may be structural elements, specification elements, usage scenarios, or any combination of these, depending on the defect list.

Experience-based Techniques

Test Technique	**Coverage** (x100 to express as a percentage of minimum test coverage)
Error guessing	When a taxonomy is used, coverage is the number of taxonomy items tested divided by the total number of taxonomy items and stating as a percentage. Without a taxonomy, coverage is limited by the experience and knowledge of the tester and the time available. Coverage is difficult to assess and varies with the capability and experience of the Test Analyst.
Checklist-based	The number of checklist items tested divided by the total number of checklist items and stating as a percentage.
Exploratory	A charter could be created to specify tasks, objectives and deliverables* then charter points completed divided by the total number of points on the charter can be expressed as a percentage.

* Note the term '*Deliverables*' has been removed from the ISTQB Glossary, but remains in the Syllabus 2019.

Exercise 7: Test Process

	One from List 1	One from List 2	One from List 3 (if appropriate)
1	**d)** System test planning occurs concurrently with	**i)** project planning	
2	**c)** Test monitoring and control continues until	**vi)** system test execution and closure are complete	
3	**e)** System test analysis and design occur concurrently with	**iv)** requirements specification, system and architectural (High-level) design specification, and component (Low-level) design specification	
4	**b)** System test environment implementation might start during	**iii)** system design though the bulk of it typically would occur concurrently with	**y)** coding and component test, with work on system test implementation activities stretching often until just days before the start of system test execution
5	**f)** System test execution begins when	**v)** the system test entry criteria are all met (or waived) which	**z)** typically means that at least component testing and often also component integration testing have met their exit criteria or definitions of 'done'
6	**g)** System test execution continues until	**vii)** the system test exit criteria are met	
7	**a)** System test completion activities occur after	**ii)** the system test exit criteria are met	

Exercise 8: Glossary Terms

Glossary List 1

i) Actual result
ii) Inspection
iii) Formal review
iv) Testability
v) Robustness

Glossary List 2

vi) Keyword-driven testing
vii) Scrum
viii) Audit
ix) Effectiveness
x) Web Content Accessibility Guidelines (WCAG)

Glossary List 3

xi) Efficiency
xii) Entry criteria
xiii) Expected result
xiv) Failure
xv) Regression testing

Glossary List 4

xvi) Metric
xvii) Smoke test
xviii) Test cycle
xix) Test oracle
xx) Severity

Glossary List 5

xxi) Test data preparation
xxii) User error protection
xxiii) High-level test case
xxiv) Test charter
xxv) Test data

Exercise 9: Test Design

Test Types box 1

Test Cases	Statement
Low-level	Can be referred to as concrete test cases
Low-level	Provide all the specific information and procedures needed for the tester to execute the test case (including any data requirements) and verify the results
Low-level	Tend to limit tester ingenuity (limit latitude) during execution
Low-level	Best when documentation is clearly defined
High-level	May result in loss of reproducibility

Test Types box 2

Test Cases	Statement
High-level	Best used when the tester is experienced with both testing and the product (experienced staff)
High-level	Also referred to as logical test cases
High-level	Formal documentation is not required (e.g. no audits)
Low-level	May require a significant amount of maintenance
High-level	May be defined early in the requirements process when requirements are not yet well-defined

Test Types box 3

Test Cases	Statement
High-level	Can be used to develop **low-level** test cases
Low-level	Best when external verification of the tests (such as audits) is required
High-level	Latitude (ingenuity) to vary data and actual steps in the business process
High-level	May provide better coverage than **low-level** test cases because they will vary each time they are executed
Low-level	Tests are easily reproducible

Exercise 10: Pairwise Testing

Step 1	Step 2	Step 3	Step 4	Step 5
D	B	E	C	A

CHECKLIST FOR EXAM PREPARATION

The following gives a summary of hints. Use these as a basis for an exam preparation checklist. Add entries to make it your own checklist.

Do not use the index to the Syllabus as a checklist for revision of the knowledge you require for the exam. The index does not include entries for all keyword terms and some important topics are missing from the index. See Chapter *Required Knowledge* for details on why using the index may not provide all the information you need.

Hints for Preparing for the Exam

Understand where to allocate your time when preparing for the exam, see Chapter *About the Exam*.

Read and re-read the ISTQB Advanced Test Analyst Syllabus 2019 V1.1, or later. Keep in mind where points about the Syllabus have been raised in this book.

Beware of using sources based on an outdated Syllabus, such as the ISTQB® 2012 Syllabus.

Use the ISTQB Glossary. Keep in mind the points about the Glossary and definitions of terms which have been raised in this book, see Chapter *Glossary and Keyword Observations*.

Know the keywords but do not be limited to these.

Use the Learning Objectives to check you have the correct level of knowledge and understanding, see Chapter *Knowledge Levels and Learning Objectives*.

Understand what is meant by the K-levels (Knowledge levels) and which questions carry the most marks.

Do not rely on just completing sample questions, your focus should be on the Learning Objectives.

Note: There may be the occasional spelling, grammar or punctuation mistake in the documents listed in the *References* Section. Do not let these distract you as they typically do not alter the sense of the text.

Hints for Questions on Test Techniques

Learn all the specified test techniques. Questions on the test techniques, Chapter 3 of the Syllabus, account for 55% (44/80 marks) of the available exam marks.

Make sure you know and understand the applicability of test techniques as given in the Syllabus.

Understand the implications of the limitations of all the test techniques, see Syllabus.

Make sure you understand and, where appropriate, can calculate the percentage coverage for test techniques, see *Revision Exercises - Answers, Exercise 6 – Minimum Test Coverage.*

Be aware that using a test technique and fulfilling coverage criteria for that technique does not necessarily mean the entire set of tests is complete, but rather that the model no longer suggests any additional tests to increase coverage based on that technique, see Chapter *Test Coverage*.

Mandatory questions on decision tables and pairwise testing carry 15% (12/80 marks). Additional knowledge beyond that included in the Syllabus is particularly recommended here, see Chapters *Decision Tables* and *Pairwise Testing.*

Pairwise Testing - Know when the minimum number of rows and columns cannot be easily calculated, see Chapter *Pairwise Testing.*

Decision Tables - Be able to create two types, tables covering combinations of conditions and tables covering individual condition outcomes, see Chapter *Decision Tables.*

Decision Tables - Recognise when given conditions are mutually exclusive and can be reduced to fewer conditions, see Chapter *Decision Tables.*

Decision Tables - Understand when the rule given in the Syllabus for calculating the number of columns needs modifying or does not apply, see Chapter *Decision Tables.*

State Transition Testing - Keep in mind that, from a particular state, when an event triggers a transition that directly returns to the original state, this is counted as one transition for 0-switch coverage or part of a transition for a higher level.

State Transition Testing - 'Round-trip coverage' applies to situations in which sequences of transitions form loops and the loops cannot contain more than one occurrence of any particular state, (except the initial/final ones).

Hints for Questions on the Test Analyst's Responsibilities

Since the 2012 Syllabus, significant changes have been made to the software characteristics the Test Analyst has responsibility for. There are added responsibilities and changes to the definitions of terms. For example, there are new and renamed terms such as, 'functional correctness', 'functional appropriateness' and 'functional completeness', see Chapter *Glossary and Keyword Observations - New Terminology for the Test Analyst's Responsibilities.* Check you know and understand these responsibilities and terms.

Nine marks are available from questions on testing software quality characteristics.

Evaluating usability – check you know techniques to do this, see Chapter *Measuring Usability*.

Hints for Questions on the Test Analyst's tasks in the Test Process

Know the four activities of the test process (test analysis, test design, test implementation and test execution) which have particular relevance for the Test Analyst to know in more depth than that required for the Foundation Level. This extends application of the test process.

Hints for Questions on the Test Analyst's tasks in Risk-based testing

Understand what is needed to be involved in the risk-based testing tasks' risk identification, risk assessment and risk mitigation.

Hints for Questions on Reviews

Know what is required for a successful review process and how to use checklists.

Keep in mind, when conducted properly, reviews can be the single most cost-effective contributor to overall delivered quality and success of the project.

Hints for Questions on the Test Tools and Automation

Know how the Test Analyst can work with developers, Test Automation Engineers and Technical Test Analysts to create test automation solutions.

ABOUT THE EXAM

The exam duration is 120 minutes. There are 40 questions with a total of 80 marks. To achieve a pass requires 52 marks (65%).

When you have the knowledge and understanding needed for the exam, go through the five-point plan below:

1	Understand the exam format
2	Understand the format of exam questions
3	Understand where marks in the exam can be gained or lost
4	Look at how to approach the questions
5	Practice questions

The basis for all exam information and questions is derived from the following documents available at the time of publication, see *References* Section.

ISTQB® Certified Tester Advanced Level Syllabus Exam Structure and Rules Test Analyst / Technical Test Analyst 2019 V1.1 19 Dec 2019

ISTQB® Exam Information - Public Version 2. 2018

Keep in mind, the ISTQB statement from the ATA Sample Exam Introduction, the '*sample questions should offer many ideas for the individual Member Boards on how to create good questions and appropriate answer sets for their examinations*'. Member Boards have available to them the ISTQB Exam Structure and Rules and the specification of question formats. Member Boards may publish their own sample questions. The details in this chapter are based on the ISTQB documents.

Overall Exam Format

The exam consists of forty multiple-choice questions. You are asked to select one option from a list of four or for a few questions two options from a list of five. The number of questions for each Learning Objective is specified, see Chapter *Knowledge Levels and Learning Objectives*. The Learning Objectives give a good indication of what to expect. All Learning Objectives have at least one question, except for TA-1.4.3, TA-1.5.1 and TA-1.6.1 where there is exactly one question on just one of these Learning Objectives.

The order of questions in the exam has not been specified, the most likely order is that used by the ISQB Sample Exam where the order of the questions matches the order of the list of Learning Objectives in the Syllabus. In an online exam, computer-generated randomization of questions results in questions, or blocks of questions, being in a different order.

Format of Exam Questions

ISTQB Exam Information - Public Version 2.0 specifies that, at Advanced Test Analyst Level, questions consist of the following elements:

Stem	A question phrase and sufficient information to select the correct response option(s).
Optional Problem Statement/Scenario	An enhancement to the stem giving a detailed description of a problem or scenario. This includes the background information required to answer the question. There may be additional details to complete the problem or scenario that are not directly needed to find the answer. Problem statements and scenarios can be used to support any question type.
Response Options	For Type A, Matching Type, and Roman Type questions four options are given, one option is the correct response. For Pick-N questions five options are given, two of these are correct. Incorrect or inferior response options are referred to as 'distracters'.

Types of Exam Questions

The four specified types of exam questions are as follows:

ISTQB® Specified Format	Details	Answer
Type A	Stem and optionally a problem statement/scenario.	Four response options a) to d). One option is correct and should be selected.
Roman Type	Stem and optionally a problem statement/scenario. Five statements, each preceded by a Roman numeral i. to v.	Four response options a) to d) for a question such as '*Which statements are true?*', the options could be: a) i, ii, iii, v b) i, ii, iv c) iv, v d) All of the tasks In the list of options, each statement will appear in at least two options and in not more than three options, in its correct truth value. One option is correct and should be selected.
Matching Type	Used to measure ability to identify the relationship or association between related items. Items in first list of four are labelled with numbers (1-4), items in second list of four are labelled with letters (A-D).	Four response options a) to d) could look like: a) 1B, 2D, 3A, 4C b) 1C, 2D, 3A, 4B c) 1C, 2A, 3B, 4D d) 1A, 2B, 3C, 4D One option is correct and should be selected.
Pick-N Type	Similar to Type A but with an additional answer option.	Five response options a) to e). Two options are correct and both should be selected. Scoring follows the rule, if both options selected are correct, the full number of points assigned to the question is awarded, otherwise no points are given.

There is no specification that all formats or a specific number of any of the specified formats must be included in the exam. The ISTQB Sample Exam uses the formats as shown in the table below where three-quarters of the questions are of Type A.

Question Type	Number of Questions in the ISTQB Sample Exam
Type A	30
Roman Type	1*
Matching Type	0
Pick-N Type	9

* Question #37 in the ISTQB launch Sample Exam is listed in the table above as Roman Type. Be aware, with only four statements and iii. and iv. only in one answer option, question #37 does not follow the specification of having five statements, each preceded by a Roman numeral and each statement appearing in at least two options and not more than three options, in its correct truth value. Also, the answer options are capitalized followed by a full stop.

The exam papers in this book, while keeping an emphasis on Type A and Pick-N Type questions as seen in the ISTQB Sample Exam, include questions in the other two permitted formats, Roman Type and Matching Type, to give wider practice of all possible formats.

Question Type	Number of Questions in Practice Exam ONE	Number of Questions in Practice Exam TWO
Type A	28	21
Roman Type	4	7
Matching Type	1	2
Pick-N Type	7	10

Where Marks can be Gained or Lost

To pass, at least 65% of the marks must be obtained. This amounts to 52 marks. Understanding the marking scheme will help in allocating the time you have available for learning and revision effort.

ISTQB Syllabus	Number of Questions in Exam	Available Marks
Chapter 1	6	10
Chapter 2	1	2
Chapter 3	17	44
Chapter 4	11	15
Chapter 5	3	6
Chapter 6	2	3
Total	**40**	**80**

Chapter 3 (*Test Techniques*) of the Syllabus accounts for 55% of the available marks. The four mandatory questions on the test techniques using decision tables and pairwise testing carry 12 marks, 15% of the total marks available. Decision tables and pairwise testing are two areas of the Syllabus where additional information is particularly desirable, both for the exam and subsequent use of the techniques. For more details, see the relevant chapters in this book.

Just over 30% of the marks are available from questions based on Chapters 1 (*The Test Analyst's Tasks in the Test Process*) and 4 (*Test Software Quality Characteristics*) of the Syllabus. The remaining marks come from Chapters 2 (*The Test Analyst's Tasks in Risk-based Testing*) 2.5%, 5 (*Reviews*) 7.5% and 6 (*Test Tools and Automation*) 3.75%.

An exam question is based on a Learning Objective. This does not preclude elements of different Learning Objectives being included. The highest K-level is typically assigned to the question.

Do not fall into the trap of thinking you need to correctly answer only 26 questions (65%) of the total of 40 questions. If you only answer 26 questions correctly and they are low scoring ones, you will not reach the pass mark.

Questions carry marks based on their K-level. The ISTBQ Exam Information - Public v2.0, 1.6.3.3 specifies, *'A K2 question is allocated 1 point, while a K3 question may score 1, 2 or 3 points, and K4 questions may score either 2 or 3 points.'* In the ISTQB Sample Exam, all K2 questions carry 1 mark, all K3 questions carry 2 marks and all K4 questions carry 3 marks. The allocation of marks in the ISTQB Sample Exam is followed as in the two Practice Exams in this book. The number of questions at each K-level and the marks assigned in the ISTQB Sample Exam and the two Practice Exams are therefore as follows:

Knowledge Level	**Marks / Question**	**Number of Questions in Exam**	**Total Marks**
K1	-	0	0
K2	1	17	17
K3	2	6	12
K4	3	17	51
Total		**40**	**80**

For the example of only answering 26 questions, consider the following:

Correctly answering all seventeen K2 questions scores 17 marks, all six K3 questions scores 12 marks plus three K4 questions which score 9 means 65% of the questions are correctly answered. However, the marks achieved give a score of 38 (47.5%) which is below that required for a pass. You must correctly answer more high scoring questions.

How to organize time in the exam is a frequent question asked by candidates wishing to attempt all questions. Based on the exam questions being in the order specified in the ISTQB® Exam Structure and Rules 2019 and the ISTQB Sample Exam order of questions, 40 marks are allocated to the first seventeen questions and 40 marks are allocated to the remaining 23 questions. When considering how you allocate your time in the exam, if you have completed question 17 after one hour (and not question 20), you may be half way depending on the order of questions.

The exam specification states, it should be possible to read and answer an exam question at K2 level in one minute or less, at K3 level in two minutes or less and at K4 level in three minutes or less. Adhering to these times suggests all questions could be read and answered on 80 minutes, leaving 40 minutes to allocate where extra time may be required.

How to Approach Exam Questions

Use steps one to four below and if this is not adequate, continue with steps five and six.

1	Read the question carefully
2	Answer the question in your mind first
3	Read all the answer options
4	Select the best answer option(s)
5	Use a process of elimination
6	When you do not know the answer

Read the question carefully

Read the question before reading the answer options. Thinking you know what a question is asking and going straight to the answer options before thoroughly reading the question can be a mistake.

Look for short phrases embedded in the question that may have a significant bearing on the answer. For example, part of question #11 in the ISTQB Sample Exam has the embedded phrase *'except Super-Saver'* which is easy to miss but has an effect on the answer.

Look for words such as 'all' or 'every' in the question as these may also have a significant bearing on the answer.

Read the questions carefully for the inclusion of negative words such as 'not/never/untrue' that will affect the answer.

Other words and phrases to look out for include, 'most appropriate', 'often', 'most often', 'best', 'most likely', 'best approach', 'best action to take', 'best strategy', 'main' and 'usually'.

Be aware questions may contain more information than is required, for example in describing a scenario. This extra information can be a distraction. Identify the key information.

Answer the question in your mind first
First answer the question in your mind before reading through the answer options. This will help prevent you from being influenced by incorrect options.

Read all the answer options
An answer option that includes words such as 'all', 'always' or 'every' must be irrefutable. If you can think of a counter-example or situation, then the answer is not correct. For example, 'Every defect should be fixed', is an incorrect statement but, 'Defects should be fixed' is more correct and might be the right choice, depending on the wording of the rest of the question.

If an answer option includes words such as 'may' or 'can be' this might be true. For example, 'Localization of any defects revealed is simplified' is refutable for some decision tables covering individual condition outcomes. However, 'Localization of any defects revealed may be simplified', could be a correct answer.

If the answer option contains words such as 'sometimes', 'some' or 'most', the answer option does not have to be completely irrefutable.

If an answer option includes a word such as '*never*' a single counterexample will indicate the answer is not correct.

Carefully check the answer options against your first answer. Adjust your answer only when you are sure you should do this.

Select the best answer option(s)
It is important to select the best answer, not just an answer option that appears to be correct. Often many answers will seem correct, but there is a best answer to the question.

Questions that require an answer that is 'best/most appropriate/most correct' may have options that are partly true and partly untrue or not true for all situations. Make sure you read all the options before selecting an answer. For example, if there is an option:

a) High-level tests make use of the Test Analyst's experience and the level of detail enables independent verification of the tests

This is not all correct, only the first part is, the second part applies to low-level tests.

For a question asking, 'Which of the statements are true?', if an answer option is, 'All of the above', do not select this if you know one of the options above is incorrect. The same applies for, 'None of the above', if you are confident at least one of the options above is true.

Remember for 'Pick-N Type' format questions, two correct options are required.

Use a process of elimination

If you are not sure which is the correct answer, rule out all the answer options you know are incorrect. Focus on the remaining answers. This greatly increases the likelihood you will select the correct answer. A process of elimination is particularly useful for questions on the number of test cases required for pairwise testing, where the minimum number of rows in a table may not be the actual number of test cases required, see Chapter *Pairwise Testing*.

When you do not know the answer

If after consideration of the question and all of the above points, you are still unsure about the options, make a guess. It will not count against your exam score. It can be counterproductive to continue to spend time on one particular question. Use your first answer choice. This does not mean your first answer is necessarily the correct answer option but is likely to be your best approach. While the multiple-choice questions are not intentionally designed to trick or confuse, they are designed to test 'knowledge and understanding'. The options will often include the most common wrong answer or answers that seem plausible but are ultimately incorrect.

Practice questions

Practice questions with appropriate time constraints. If you are not attempting a complete paper, look at the points for an indication of the likely K-level and how long to spend on a question. It should be possible to read and answer a question at K2 level (1 point) in one minute or less, at K3 (typically 2 points) in two minutes and at K4 (typically 3 points) in three minutes.

Only use reliable sources for practice questions. Be aware, some questions from online sources may be relevant, others may no longer be in the 2019 Syllabus.

Try the ISTQB Sample Exam. Add up your score.

When you are confident, try Practice Exam One in this book.

PRACTICE EXAM ONE QUESTIONS

40 Questions – 2019 Syllabus
Time allowed 120 minutes
52 / 80 marks are required for a Pass

Question #1 (1 Point)
Whatever the Software Development Life Cycle (SDLC) being used, which of the following statements is the Test Analyst's best approach?

a) Determine the most effective role and the proper moment of involvement rather than depend on the definition of the test model
b) Be involved as laid down by the definition of the test model being used
c) Participate in high-level planning at the beginning of the project and then conduct test analysis, design, implementation, execution and completion tasks
d) Participate in high-level planning at the beginning of the project and then conduct test analysis, design and execution

Select ONE option

Question #2 (1 Point)
You are working on a project where the application of test techniques has been identified in the test strategy. Consider the following:

i. Identification of test conditions
ii. Reduction of the likelihood of omitting important test conditions
iii. Definition of more precise and accurate test conditions
iv. Review of identified test conditions with the stakeholders to ensure testing is aligned with the goals of the project
v. Identification of the test data to support test conditions and test cases

During the test analysis process, application of test techniques may be used to support which of the objectives above?

a) i, ii, iii and iv
b) ii, iv and v
c) i and iii
d) i, ii, iii, iv and v

Select ONE option

Question #3 (1 Point)

During test design, for the most successful outcome, the Test Analyst considers input from stakeholders. Consider the following:

i. Developers should not review the test conditions as there is a risk they will code to particular tests and this can result in problems later on. Understanding the tests should always be left to the testers. Developers should code to the documented specifications. Users should be involved as they will be using the system's functionality

ii. Assessors such as auditors should not be involved in reviewing test conditions because assessors should remain independent

iii. Communicators, such as writers of manuals, training materials and other documents, will provide little or no benefit and may introduce unnecessary delays. They should rely on project specifications and other documentation.

iv. Risk identification is best (in terms of time required and coverage) done by experienced testers with input from the system administrators as it is, they who will be running the system when it is deployed and responsible for its availability

v. Third-party partners, external to the company, who are involved in the development process. should not be involved in reviewing test conditions drawn up by the company's direct employees

Which is the best overall assessment of the statements above?

a) i, iv are true ii, iii, v is false
b) All of the options are true
c) All of the options are false
d) Another answer not listed here

Select ONE option

Question #4 (3 Points)

A delivery company has started a new project 'Drop A Pack', DAP, to expand its service with the introduction of a wider range of trucks with varying load capacities. The project is in two parts, DAP1 and DAP2.

DAP1 - The software optimizes use of the trucks in terms of total volume, type and weight of goods a truck can transport, this must conform to the vehicle manufacturers' specifications. The software also schedules a driver with the correct qualifications for the size of the vehicle and with sufficient hours permitted under legal regulations to be able to fulfil delivery on the required day. The project must meet the requirements of the company's finance department. The project team for DAP1 has testers who are business users with significant domain experience, but no formal testing experience.

DAP2 - The second part of the project is the user interface. The customer will be able to input their requirements in terms of volume, type and weight of goods, collection and delivery locations and have an indicative price. Testing of this will be done by well-trained Agile testers who have previously worked on marketing software for this company.

As a Test Analyst, you have been asked for your input. Which is the best strategy to adopt?

a) DAP1 and DAP2 test cases should be low-level with well-documented procedures and traceability to requirements. This will provide a consistent test strategy for the whole project

b) DAP1 test cases should be high-level. Testers are business users who know the business rules and calculations so there is no need for detailed documentation. DAP2 test cases should low-level level with documented procedures and traceability

c) DAP1 test cases should be low-level with detailed documentation. DAP2 test cases should be high-level, allowing the testers flexibility in varying the details to achieve higher coverage

d) DAP1 and DAP2 test cases should high-level as both the business users and the Agile testers have significant experience

Select ONE option

Question #5 (3 Points)

As a Test Analyst, you are working with an FX e-currency exchange application that allows users to submit funds for conversion from one currency to another one. The application processes the conversion request through a number of phases; checks the user is authorised, funds are available and the current conversion rate before the execution of the transaction. The application must be fully compliant with FCA exchange regulations. To make sure the project is delivered on time, additional experienced testers are employed on contract. These testers do not have detailed domain knowledge. Test automation will not be used at this stage but is in the long-term plan for future updates.

Which is the most correct statement for the level of testing required?

a) High-level as the contract staff have testing experience and it will be more straightforward to automate the tests in the future
b) High-level as the testing will provide better risk coverage and the contract staff have testing experience with this application
c) Low-level as this will allow high-level tests to be developed in the future which can then be used to support test automation in the future
d) Low-level as this allows audit verification and it will be more straightforward in the future to automate the tests

Select ONE option

Question #6 (1 Point)

You are in the test implementation phase of a project for an e-commerce application and are using a risk-based strategy blended with iterative testing.
Consider the following tasks:

i. Create input and environment data to load into the databases and other such repositories
ii. Verify procedures that gather data for evaluating status against exit criteria
iii. Check those responsible for the creation and maintenance of the environment are known and available
iv. Identify test cases that can be grouped together
v. Coordinate with the development team to ensure that the software is released for testing in a testable order

For the test implementation phase, which of the following is true?

a) Test Analyst should do i and iv, Test Manager is responsible for ii, iii and v
b) Test Analyst should do ii and iv, user is responsible for providing input and environment data i. Test Manager is responsible for iii and v
c) Test Analyst should do ii, iii and v, tasks i. and iv. should have been in the test analysis phase
d) Test Analyst should do all the tasks listed

Select ONE option

Question #7 (2 Points)

As a Test Analyst, you are testing a banking application that allows users to add certain data fields (A1, A2, A3), change data (C1, C2, C3) and delete data (D1, D2). These tasks have been risk-assessed as shown in the table below:

	Task	Impact	Likelihood
A1	Add	High	High
A2	Add	High	Low
A3	Add	Medium	Medium
C1	Change	High	High
C2	Change	Medium	Low
C3	Change	Low	Low
D1	Delete	Medium	Medium
D2	Delete	High	High

Which is the correct order for risk-level depth-first testing?

a) A1, C1, D1, A2, C2, D2, A3, C3
b) A1, C1, D2, A2, A3, D1, C2, C3
c) A1, A2, C1, C2, D1, D2, A3, C3
d) A1, A2, A3, C1, C2, C3, D1, D2

Select ONE option

Question #8 (3 Points)

You are testing an application for an airline company that gives incentives to frequent flyers. Regular (up to and including 10 sectors flown) entitles the passenger to free beverages on-board. Gold (11 or more sectors flown up to 19) entitles the passenger to use of a lounge. Platinum (20 or more sectors flown up to 29) entitles the passenger to an additional free cabin bag. Executive Platinum (30 or more sectors flown up to a maximum of 50) entitles the passenger to priority boarding. The incentives are additive. For example, a platinum level passenger would have free beverages onboard, use of a lounge and an additional free cabin bag. Zero sectors are possible where these are typically on feeder flights for long-distance flights. Negative sectors are invalid. Sectors are always integer values. Depending on the fare paid, bonus miles are awarded. Standard Economy = 1.5 x bonus miles, Business Class = 2 x bonus miles, First Class = 4 x bonus miles. Standby tickets attract no bonus, only the exact number of miles.

How many test cases are needed for 100% minimum equivalence partition test coverage?

a) 6 partitions for the sector tests, 4 partitions for the fare type
b) 4 partitions for the sector tests, 6 partitions for the fare type
c) 8 partitions for the sector tests, 6 partitions for the fare type
d) 4 partitions to cover both sectors and fare type in the same test cases

Select ONE option

Question #9 (3 Points)

You working on an application that monitors a controlled environment. The temperature is measured to 0.5°C accuracy. The temperature must not drop to below -5°C and must not reach 15°C or higher. If this does occur, a warning alarm must be sounded. If the temperature is equal to either 4.0°C or -5.0°C or any value between these two temperatures, a green light is displayed. If the temperature is greater than 4.0°C, a yellow light is displayed.

Which of the following would provide the best 2-value boundary analysis for 100% coverage?

a) -5°C, -6°C, 4°C, 4°C, 15°C, 16°C
b) -5.0°C, -4.5°C, 3.5°C, 4.0°C,15.0°C,15.5°C
c) -4.5°, 5C, -5.5°C, 3.5°C, 4°C, 4.5°C, 14.5°C, 15°C, 15.5°C
d) -5°C, -5.5°C, 4°C, 4.5°C, 14.5°C, 15°C

Select ONE option

Question #10 (3 Points)

You are testing a hotel room booking application. There are two price ranges, the higher range is used for rooms booked for April to October, the lower range is for November to March. The exceptions to this are over Christmas, New Year and Public holidays, which are always charged at the higher rates regardless of when they occur. Within each price range, the hotel has three rates corresponding to the room type, single, double or family room. The hotel is in the commercial area of a major city and finds it regularly attracts business clients for Monday through Thursday and also some tourist couples during the high season. To increase room bookings, the hotel is launching a new initiative to attract more tourists with families. During the high-price season, the hotel is offering a 15% discount on family rooms at the weekends. During the low-price season, but excluding Christmas, New Year and Public holidays, the hotel is offering a 10% discount on family rooms for any weekday or weekend bookings and 10% discount for double rooms at weekends.

Using decision table testing covering combinations of conditions, what is the minimum number of test cases are required to cover all non-redundant and feasible decision combinations?

a) 6
b) 7
c) 8
d) 9

Select ONE option

Question #11 (3 Points)

You are working on an update to the billing component of an application used for a company that sells building supplies on account to trade customers. The company wishes to give discounts if payments are made within 14 days of the month end where the discount is 2%. If the monthly amount is over £500, this discount is increased to 3%. When all orders have been placed online there is an additional 5% discount. You are considering using either a decision table covering all combinations of conditions or a decision table covering all individual condition outcomes.

How many more test cases are required for testing all combinations of conditions above the number for testing all individual condition outcomes?

a) 2
b) 4
c) 6
d) 8

Select ONE option

Question #12 (3 Points)

An oil drilling company has developed a system to report on the depth of the drilling equipment and its rotational speed of drilling based on the following state table. A signal is required from the drilling equipment to allow the calculation to be performed.

	Depth	Rotational Speed	Update	No Signal
Display	Calculate	Calculate		
Calculate	-	-	Display	Retry
Retry	Calculate	Calculate		End

Starting from display, how many test cases are needed to achieve 100% minimum 0-switch coverage?

a) 5
b) 4
c) 3
d) 2

Select ONE option

Question #13 (3 Points)

You are testing payment software. If the user enters valid payment details (card number and elements of password), the order is placed and the user is taken to the order confirmation page. With invalid payment details, the user is taken to a payment rejected page with a warning that only one further attempt to enter payment details is allowed. If the payment details are invalid on the second attempt, the user is taken to the close-out page and asked to contact their bank.

Which of the following state tables correctly shows the state changes starting from the payment requested state?

a)

Start State	Event	Condition	Action	End State
Payment requested	Payment details entered	Valid	Order placed	Order confirmation

b)

Start State	Event	Condition	Action	End State
Payment requested	Payment details entered	Valid	Order placed	Order confirmation
Payment requested	Payment details entered	Invalid	Order not placed	Payment rejected

c)

Start State	Event	Condition	Action	End State
Payment requested	Payment details entered	Valid	Order placed	Order confirmation
Payment requested	Payment details entered	Invalid	Order not placed	Payment rejected
Payment rejected	Alternative payment details entered	Valid	Order placed	Order confirmation

d)

Start State	Event	Condition	Action	End State
Payment requested	Payment details entered	Valid	Order placed	Order confirmation
Payment requested	Payment details entered	Invalid	Order not placed	Payment rejected
Payment rejected	Alternative payment details entered	Valid	Order placed	Order confirmation
Payment rejected	Alternative payment details entered	Invalid	Order not placed	Closeout

Select ONE option

Question #14 (1 Point)

As a Test Analyst, you are working with an application for selling cars. Customers can choose a new car paint (red, white or blue), the interior trim (leather, grey or tweed cloth) and diesel or petrol engine.

You use a classification tree to set up the following test cases:

	Colour			**Trim**			**Engine**	
Test Case	Red	White	Blue	Leather	Grey Cloth	Tweed Cloth	Diesel	Petrol
1	o			o			o	
2	o				o			o
3	o					o	o	
4		o		o				o
5		o			o		o	
6		o				o		o
7			o	o			o	
8			o		o			o
9			o			o	o	

Which of the following best describes the model where 100% minimum test coverage is achieved using the classification tree above?

a) Singleton
b) Pairs
c) Triples
d) 100% coverage is not achieved

Select ONE option

Question #15 (3 Points)

A shower company offers the non-interacting options given below. These can be ordered using an online application. Types of shower available are; electric, mixer (uses hot and cold water supplies) and thermostatic valve shower. Showerhead types are hand-held only, showerhead on a slide, fixed head wall-mounted, fixed ceiling-mounted, showerhead combined with side body jets. The customer can also order a shower enclosure with either a sliding panel or folding door. You are tasked with creating test cases.

How many tests are required for 100% pairwise coverage?

a) 15
b) 5
c) 10
d) 30

Select ONE option

Question #16 (3 Points)

You are working on a new website for a retailer. The client requires the website to be available on Microsoft Windows 10™, macOS® or Android™ tablet and with browsers; Microsoft Edge™ for MS Windows 10 PCs, Safari® (but not for Android tablets) or Chrome browser. Display output can be to a local screen for all devices or to a large external screen for Windows 10 and macOS only. You are conducting pairwise testing. You have been given the following test cases to review:

Test Case	Operating System	Browser	Screen Type
1	MS Windows 10	Microsoft Edge	External
2	MS Windows 10	Safari	Local
3	macOS	Safari	External
4	macOS	Chrome	Local
5	Android	Safari	Local
6	Android	Chrome	External

Based on the given information, which of the following are not true for giving the best coverage?

a) A test case is required for MS Windows/Chrome/External Screen
b) A test case is required for MS Windows/Safari/External Screen
c) A test case is required for MS Windows/ Microsoft Edge /Local Screen
d) Test case 5 should be corrected to Android/Chrome/Local Screen
e) Test 6 is not required

Select TWO options

Question #17 (3 Points)

As a Test Analyst, you are working on an application for a University. You have the following use case:

USE CASE: Seminar Enrolment Use case ID: UC-2727
Purpose: Student is enrolling for a seminar
Actors: Student, Enrolment software
Preconditions: Student eligibility database, list of seminars and their prerequisites
Special requirement: Display reason for enrolment failure

User	System
1. Inputs student number	2. Verifies eligibility to enrol in seminars (E01)
	3. Displays a list of available seminars
4. Selects seminar (E02)	5. Validates student has the mandatory prerequisites (E03)
	6. Displays seminar in the student's existing schedule
	7. Asks 'continue or select different seminar?'
8. Confirms 'Continue' (E04)	9. Enrols student in the seminar
	10. Asks if printed statement of enrolment required
11. Responds 'Yes' (E05)	12. Prints enrolment confirmation statement

E01: Student is not eligible to enrol in seminars
System informs 'not eligible'. Use case ends
E02: Student decides not to continue
Use case ends.
E03: Student does not have the prerequisites
System informs 'prerequisites not met' next to seminar listing
Use case continues at step 4
E04: Student selects different seminar, (E02)
Use case continues at step 4
E05: Printed confirmation is not required
Use case ends

You have completed the following tests:
Test case 1: 1, 2, 3, 4, 5, 6, 7, 8, 10, 11, 12
Test case 2: 1, 2, E01

What percentage of minimum test coverage has been achieved?

a) 66%
b) 40%
c) 33%
d) 50%

Select ONE option

Question #18 (3 Points)

You have been brought in to work on an application used by a grocery store. Customers may choose to use point from a loyalty card to receive discounted goods. You have the following use case:

USE CASE: Point of Sale
Actors: Customer, self-checkout terminal
Precondition: Customer has arrived at checkout with goods
Post-conditions: Customer has purchased goods and received receipt
Flow:

Customer	System
1. Scans goods	2. Displays line item details and running total
3. Enters payment details	4. Validates payment information and records (E1)
5. Scans store loyalty card (E2)	6. Adds loyalty points to card
7. Elects to use loyalty points	8. Updates payment required
	9. Updates inventory and issues receipt

Exception	System
E1 Invalid payment	Asks for payment details to be re-input. Details validated and recorded with success, use case continues. If second attempt fails, a third attempt is allowed, use case ends if third attempt fails.
E2 No loyalty card	Offers sign up for card. If customer does not require card, use case continues at 9. customer signs up for loyalty card. Use case continues at 6
E3 No use of loyalty points	Use case continues at 9

How many test cases are required for 100% minimum use case test coverage?

a) 3
b) 5
c) 6
d) 4

Select ONE option

Question #19 (3 Points)

As a Test Analyst, you working on an application that allocates annual leave. There are two types of contract, full-time and part-time. Full-time employees receive 28 days. Part-time employees receive a pro-rata number of days. New rules are being introduced for extra holiday based on time served in full years. Employees with at least 20 years of service receive an additional two days. An employee, who has at least 10 but less than 20 years of service, will receive one extra day. In any year, an employee uses all their leave or can carry forward up to five days to the following year. Arrangements for maternity or paternity leave are remaining the same. Minimal changes to the user interface and the number of screens an employee needs to view are specified so that employees can easily continue to access the application to check leave allowance.

Adopting which two of the following together would provide the best strategy for achieving acceptable test coverage?

a) State transition testing
b) Decision table testing
c) Boundary value analysis
d) Use case testing
e) Pairwise testing

Select TWO options

Question #20 (3 Points)

As a Test Analyst, you are working on a new front end for a Social Security government application that determines if the user is eligible for state benefits. The application must be usable by the people applying for benefits. There are many areas where the application requests additional information, depending on the answer to a particular question. For example, one question asks, 'How many dependent children do you have living with you?' If the response is a number greater than zero, the application moves to a screen to prompt for details on the number of children, their ages and confirmation or otherwise that they are in full-time education. The application asks if anyone in the household is in paid employment, either full-time or part-time, as hours worked are taken into consideration. If the answer is 'Yes', the application moves to another screen to prompt for information on each person's employment hours and pay.

Which of the following are the best test techniques to use?

a) State transition
b) Pairwise testing
c) Decision table
d) Use case
e) Boundary analysis

Select TWO options

Question #21 (1 Point)

Which of the following statements are not true for experience-based testing?

a) Testing may not always be entirely dynamic, tests may be created at a different time to test execution
b) Using experience-based techniques, test execution and test evaluation are concurrent tasks
c) In situations where system documentation is poor, experienced-based techniques may be a good alternative to more structured approaches
d) Without a taxonomy of specific defects, coverage using error guessing is not limited by the knowledge of the tester ability and the time available
e) Testing is not effective when operational failures are being analyzed

Select TWO options

Question #22 (2 Points)

As a Test Analyst, you are working with a new application for purchasing washbasin taps and plugs. The system accepts a specified range of credit cards. There are a variety of taps, some use a lever-action, others have a turning action. There are standard metal or plastic plugs with chains and pop-up/pop-down plugs which do not require a chain. The user inputs his requirements, the application works out the correct code(s) for the product(s) and then sends the details to order fulfilment where the user's payment is processed. The project has a limited budget.

Which of the following would provide the best test charter to use for guiding the testing?

a) Purchase a variety of taps and a variety of plugs using both valid and invalid credit cards
b) Log in and buy a few taps and plugs and cancel before purchase to minimize time and cost of testing
c) Log in, search, buy a tap and plug then remove these from the shopping cart. Select more items and delete from shopping cart
d) Emulate a user buying two taps and one plug

Select ONE option

Question #23 (1 Point)

You are preparing tests for User Acceptance Testing (UAT) of an online ordering application. There is a large set of existing test cases that have been used previously for functional suitability testing and you would like to use these as a guideline for the UAT testers while allowing the testers to determine the data and exact steps to use.

Which of the following techniques would be most suitable to use in this situation?

a) Exploratory
b) Error guessing
c) Use case
d) Checklist

Select ONE option

Question #24 (3 Points)

As a Test Analyst, you are working on an updated version of a conference room booking application that has been in production for five years. Throughout that time, a large defect database has been built up, including defects found during testing and defects that escaped into production. The purpose of the update is to fix a number of the defects. Staff using the application are well-trained on using the application. No additional training is planned for the update release. From previous testing experience of this application, the test team is aware of many of the problem areas.

Which one of the following would be the best strategy to adopt?

a) Use the legacy requirements documents as a test oracle to ensure existing functionality is not broken by new updates
b) Apply experience-based testing, focussing on the areas where the product. experiences the heaviest usage based on established usage models
c) Create a new defect taxonomy and apply defect-based testing
d) Work with testers not experienced with this product to provide a fresh assessment of the updated application

Select ONE option

Question #25 (1 Point)

You are testing an application that handles high volume and high-value bank transfers to accounts within the bank and to external accounts, some of which are overseas. There are many systems the application has to interact with. The system must work accurately and in compliance with the regulations for money transfers.

Which of the following lists the techniques that would make up the most appropriate approach for testing this application?

a) Error guessing, exploratory testing, decision tables
b) Decision tables, usability testing, state transition testing
c) Decision tables, use case testing, state transition testing
d) Checklist testing, state transition testing, user case

Select ONE option

Question #26 (1 Point)

You are working on an application for a car rental company. Customers can rent cars provided they have a valid driving licence and meet the registration requirements. The condition of the car is agreed, recorded before release and checked on return to establish if any new problems have occurred for which the customer may be charged. Cars are rented with a full tank of fuel and if returned with less than a full tank, an appropriate charge is calculated and added to the bill.

Which of the following indicate functional appropriateness testing?

a) Error messages that appear when the registration fails must be sufficiently informative and understandable to identify the reason registration fails. This testing is to be conducted during the later stages of integration testing
b) The number of characters in a customer's address. This testing is to be conducted during the later stages of integration testing
c) Completing the vehicle checks, agreeing and recording faults before the car is released and making a comparison when the vehicle is returned. This testing is to be conducted during the later stages of integration testing
d) When returning the vehicle, the calculated fuel cost is proportional to the amount of fuel needed to refill the tank to full. This testing is to be conducted during the later stages of integration testing

Select ONE option.

Question #27 (1 Point)

You have been brought in to work with a new component being added to an application used by a footwear store. When a customer selects a shoe from the store display, staff use the application to check availability of the required size being in the storeroom by entering the appropriate 10-digit code for the shoes. The application confirms (or otherwise) the shoes needed are in stock. If the shoes are available, the process ends with the application displaying the retail price. A mistake in entering the code can lead to checking for an incorrect pair of shoes. The new specified component will streamline the process and avoid some of the mistakes made previously. It will not require staff to enter the shoe code as they will take an image of the shoe on display using an Apple iPad™, the application will identify the shoe and send the correct code for the database enquiry. The company requires the update to be available within a very limited time-scale.

Based on the information above, which of the following statements is most correct?

a) As part of functional correctness testing, testing is required for checking staff correctly use the iPad, shoe identification is made correctly and the correct price is calculated

b) As part of functional appropriateness testing, testing is required for checking the shoe identification and as part of functional correctness testing the correct price is generated

c) As part of functional appropriateness testing, testing is required for establishing the process is streamlined, the image on an iPad leads to having the correct shoe identification of the shoe and functional completeness testing is required to check availability

d) As part of functional correctness testing, testing is required for checking the image on an iPad leads to the correct identification of the shoe and functional completeness includes testing for the display of the retail price

Select ONE option

Question #28 (1 Point)

The Test Analyst is responsible for testing certain quality characteristics which are further qualified with sub-characteristics. Consider the following statements and the list of sub-characteristics:

1. Adherence to implied requirements and conducted at any test level
2. Focus includes how information that has been exchanged is used. Conducted during component integration and system testing
3. Usually conducted during system testing, but may also be conducted during the later stages of integration testing
4. Compares the requirements that have undergone a test process with those that have been implemented

A. Functional correctness testing
B. Functional appropriateness testing
C. Functional completeness testing
D. Interoperability

Which is the best option below for linking the two lists?

a) 1B, 2D, 3C, 4A
b) 1A, 2C, 3B, 4D
c) 1C, 2D, 3B, 4A
d) 1A, 2D, 3B, 4C

Select ONE option

Question #29 (1 Point)

When considering usability testing, which two statements are not necessarily true?

a) Heuristic evaluation examines the user interface and assesses its compliance with recognised principles
b) Usability reviews are always more effective when there is a detailed narrative description of the functionality provided by a particular screen rather than a sample screenshot
c) When prototypes are developed, the Test Analyst should work with the prototype and help developers evolve the prototype by incorporating user feedback into the design
d) Usability test scenarios always measure functional outcomes
e) SUMI and WAMMI surveys allow for benchmarking against a database of previous usability measurements

Select TWO options

Question #30 (1 Point)

You are working on an application for a railway company. Users log in and purchase travel tickets. There are options for standard and off-peak tickets. Some users have railcards that give discounts on standard tickets. Tickets can be bought for the same day or for any time up to one month in advance. You have a team of five testers who have no previous experience with the application. You have been asked to look at usability for task completion. You have designed the following test cases:

Test 1 Purchase an off-peak ticket for later today
Test 2 Purchase a standard ticket for travel tomorrow
Test 3 Purchase a standard ticket for travel one week later with a travel card
Test 4 Amend the ticket in Test 3 to change the date of travel to two weeks later

Three testers complete all tasks in 3 minutes. One tester completes tests 1, 2 and 3 in 4 minutes and fails to complete test 4. One tester fails to complete any task.

Which of the following is most correct?

a) Fifteen tasks out of twenty have been completed, so the relative efficiency is 75%
b) Three out of five testers completed all tasks, so the satisfaction is 60%
c) Three out of five testers completed all tasks, so the efficiency is 60%
d) Fifteen tasks out of twenty have been completed, so the effectiveness is 75%

Select ONE option

Question #31 (1 Point)

You are working on an updated ordering application used by a car repair depot. The depot in the United Kingdom repairs German cars that have been brought into the UK. Some spares are held in the UK. If a required spare is not available in the UK, the application passes the request to the German manufacturer's system from where it is sourced and dispatched. Non-urgent orders have S for standard delivery (5 working days) added at the end of their eight-digit code number, urgent orders have R for Rapid delivery (2 working days).

Which of the following is the most correct for the defect to be classified as interoperability?

a) A few parts ordered which have come from the UK depot have not been the latest version despite the latest part number being input correctly on the order
b) A few parts coming from Germany with the correct order numbers have been fitted successfully but have later failed because the parts were designed for German left-hand drive cars and not for UK right-hand drive cars
c) Parts are not always arriving in the UK on time. When a part is dispatched from the German depot, either S for Schnell (fast) delivery or R for Regular, an e-mail is automatically sent to the depot notifying them. The depot then contacts the customer, arranging for them to bring their car in for the repair as appropriate to the expected delivery time
d) Some German employees have found the software difficult to use

Select ONE option

Question #32 (1 Point)

Which of the following statements is most correct when considering interoperability testing?

a) Interactions may not all be specified in the requirements documents
b) Testing is not required for commercial off-the-shelf (COTS) products and tools as these products and tools will conform to industry wide-standards and have already been tested
c) When software can automatically detect the communications needs of the system with which it interacts, testing is not required
d) Testing is performed during system testing and acceptance testing

Select ONE option

Question #33 (1 Point)

If the software cannot be installed, then it is of no use.

Which of the following statements is most correct for what the Test Analyst should do?

a) Test installation, back-up and restore procedures sufficiently, this may mean repeating tests as final installation process may not be in place until a later stage
b) The Test Analyst is not responsible for installation testing but should test both back-up and restore procedures sufficiently
c) Save time and effort by testing installation, back-up and restore procedures at the start of the project and then move on to other testing
d) The Test Analyst is not responsible for testing back-up and restore procedures. These are the responsibility of operations staff

Select ONE option

Question #34 (3 Points)

You are working with an Android app that provides users with live sports streaming and summary reports of score-lines from earlier sporting events. By supporting as many screen formats as possible, the app can be made available to the greatest number of users on different devices. The layout needs to be flexible to adapt to different screen sizes and orientations as well as handling window configuration changes, such as multi-window mode. There is a tight schedule to get the work done. You have been asked by your Test Manager to specifically look at adaptability and functionality testing.

Given the information above, which of the following statements are most correct?

a) Adaptability tests may be performed in conjunction with installability tests and can be followed by functional tests to detect faults which may have been introduced in adapting software to a different environment

b) After adaptability testing has been completed, functional appropriateness tests are not needed

c) Adaptability testing is the responsibility of the Technical Test Analyst and not the responsibility of the Test Analyst so you should ask your Test Manager to involve a Technical Analyst to test adaptability and you will concentrate on functional testing. The involvement of an additional tester will help achieve the deadline

d) Adaptability tests are best performed in conjunction with security tests, making it more appropriate for a Technical Test Analyst to do the testing

e) Adaptability testing involves using a selection of functional test cases which exercise various components present in the environment

Select TWO options

Question #35 (3 Points)
As a Test Analyst, you are working on a new updated version of an application for which there is a new format of the database. If the database is not replaced, the new version of the application will fail when trying to access the old database format. During the installation of the new database, you encounter the following warning:

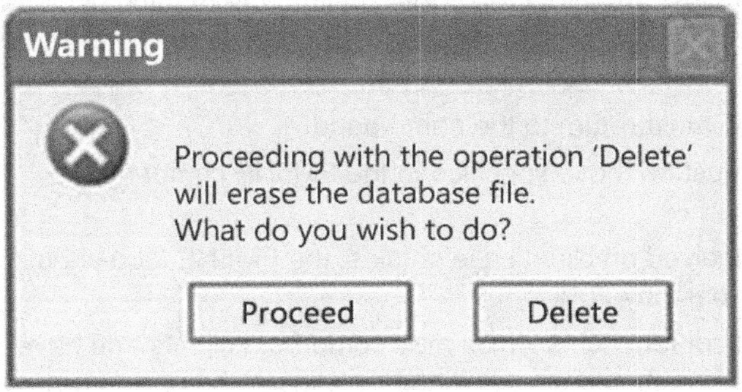

Which of the following is the best action for you to take?

a) Check that the requirements specification states a warning should be given and when you confirm that it does, take no further action
b) Raise a defect report to update the requirements specification because the new database is essential and there should not be an option to avoid installing it
c) Raise a report for a functional correctness defect
d) Raise a report for an interoperability defect

Select ONE option

Question #36 (2 Points)

You are a Test Analyst working on an application to be used by a management consultancy, FM5NE, to launch its services.

Extract from Test Requirements document based on marketing document A19 section 2020

R2020-123: The FM5NE company logo must appear at the upper right corner of each page and must meet the regulations for consistency in the ratio height to width dimensions specified in the FM5NE company Style Guide 2019/73e

R2020-125: Clicking on the FM5NE logo must return to the home page

R2020-123: Colours used for the logo must be those specified in the FM5NE company Style Guide 2019/73e

R2020-126: When displaying articles received on client case studies, the FM5NE logo should be emphasized by extending its base by 20%

R2020-127: When displaying published content items which may come from clients and have their logos present, the FM5NE logo should always match or exceed the size of any other logo displayed

R2020-128: The FM5NE logo must not be embedded in any photograph or image displayed

You have been asked to participate in a requirements review. For your preparation, you are using a checklist which includes the following:

i. Must have a unique identifier
ii. Standards used must show a version number
iii. Uses consistent and clear terminology
iv. Must be testable
v. Must show traceability to one or more business/marketing requirements

Which of the checklist items are not respected?

a) i, ii, iii
b) ii, iv, v
c) i, iii, iv, v
d) i, iii

Select ONE option

Question #37 (2 Points)

As a Test Analyst, you have been given the following screenshots from the development team as a basis for a user story. There is a tight time-schedule for testing to be completed.

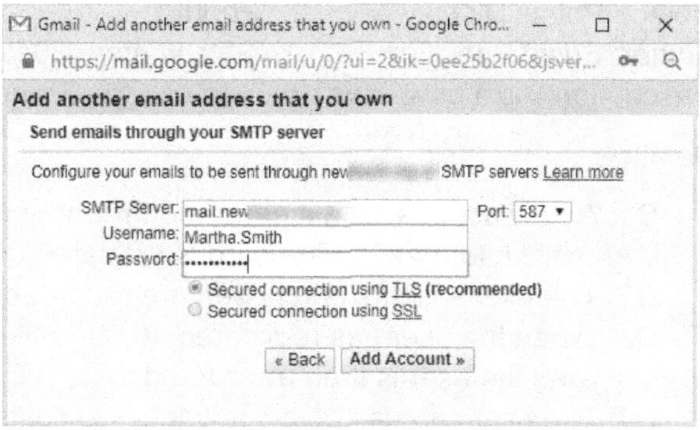

Gmail™ and logo are registered trademarks of Google LLC.

You are using the following checklist. Which of the checklist items has not been met by this user story?

a) Given from the user's perspective
b) Clearly defined and distinct
c) Prioritised
d) Independent of any other

Select ONE option

Question #38 (2 Points)

You are reviewing the following user story:

Document: Req. Spec 101-A Version: 0.23 System: Bookkeeping TA-AB1 Subsystem: 2a15
Object: Points Display Priority:
Author: Susie Specifier Date written: 2019-03-15
Description: As a new user I want to use the Frequent Flyer program to access benefits.

Detail:

D1: A new user can register for the Frequent Flyer program at standard level after entering valid information. The card is activated when the first flight is purchased
D2: The user's flights purchased are recorded and points are awarded based on the miles flown
D3: When the user has registered 10,000 miles, membership is upgraded to premium level and the user is then awarded double points on miles flown
D4: The user can use points towards the costs of some flights provided they do not fall in certain times of the year, the blackout periods for the scheme
D5: If the user's points fall below 10,000 miles, membership is downgraded to standard level and one point is given for every mile flown

Using a checklist, which two of the following are not met?

a) Story is prioritized
b) No dependencies between this component and software available for other stories that could make testing this component not viable
c) Acceptance criteria are clearly defined and testable
d) Follows the commonly used format, 'who' / 'what' / 'why'
e) Written from the view of the user

Select TWO options

Question #39 (2 Points)

You are working on a project where you have created the required keyword data for automated testing. The automation scripts, that use these keywords, have been written by the developer. You are responsible for executing the test cases. There is a failure. You have checked the expected result is correctly specified and this is not a false negative. You have checked the keywords and established there is no problem there.

What is the best action you should take next?

a) Raise a defect report for the developer to check the automated script
b) Manually run the same test with the same data as the one that failed. When you find this does not fail, report the test as passed and take no further action
c) Manually run the same test with the same data as the one that failed. When you find this does not fail, report the test as passed and make a note for testers to be aware of this anomaly in future testing
d) Manually run the same test with the same data as the one that failed. When you find this does not fail, review the sequence of steps that led up to the failure to determine if the problem occurred in a previous step but did not surface until later in processing

Select ONE option

Question #40 (1 Point)

Test tools can improve the efficiency and functional correctness of the test effort.

Which of the following is most true for automated tools for test execution?

a) Tools can be used to run tests overnight, freeing up a Test Analyst's time and effort. Their use results in test execution time being more predictable
b) Tools can automate all manual tests and perform tasks such as large data validation that would be impossible to run manually due to the amount of data involved
c) Written in low-level instructions, tools are of greater benefit to a Test Analyst than those written in a high-level language. They provide detail that makes it easier to write test cases
d) Return on investment for tools is highest when testing the functionality of new features of an application

Select ONE option

PRACTICE EXAM ONE ANSWERS

40 Answers

Question Number	Correct Answer	LO	K-Level	Points
1	a	TA-1.2.1	K2	1
2	a	TA-1.3.1	K2	1
3	c	TA-1.4.1	K2	1
4	c	TA-1.4.2	K4	3
5	d	TA-1.4.2	K4	3
6	d	TA-1.5.1	K2	1
7	b	TA-2.1.1	K3	2
8	a	TA-3.2.1	K4	3
9	d	TA-3.2.2	K4	3
10	c	TA-3.2.3	K4	3
11	b	TA-3.2.3	K4	3
12	c	TA-3.2.4	K4	3
13	b	TA-3.2.4	K4	3
14	a	TA-3.2.5	K2	1
15	a	TA-3.2.6	K4	3
16	b, e	TA-3.2.6	K4	3*
17	d	TA-3.2.7	K4	3
18	d	TA-3.2.7	K4	3
19	b, c	TA-3.2.8	K4	3*
20	a, d	TA-3.2.8	K4	3*

Question Number	Correct Answer	LO	K-Level	Points
21	d, e	TA-3.3.1	K2	1*
22	a	TA-3.3.2	K3	2
23	d	TA-3.3.3	K2	1
24	a	TA-3.4.1	K4	3
25	c	TA-4.2.1	K2	1
26	a	TA-4.2.2	K2	1
27	d	TA-4.2.2	K2	1
28	d	TA-4.2.3	K2	1
29	b, d	TA-4.2.4	K2	1*
30	d	TA-4.2.4	K2	1
31	c	TA-4.2.5	K2	1
32	a	TA-4.2.5	K2	1
33	a	TA-4.2.6	K2	1
34	a, e	TA-4.2.7	K4	3*
35	c	TA-4.2.7	K4	3
36	d	TA-5.2.1	K3	2
37	c	TA-5.2.2	K3	2
38	a, b	TA-5.2.2	K3	2*
39	d	TA-6.2.1	K3	2
40	a	TA-6.3.1	K2	1

* If both options selected are correct, the full number of points assigned to the question are awarded, otherwise no points are given.

Question	Correct Answer	Explanation / Rationale	Learning Objective K-level	Points
Q1	a	a) is the correct answer. Option b) is not the best approach as it is important the Test Analyst works towards the proper moment of involvement rather than depend on the definition of a set model. c) is not the best option as the Syllabus does not include a focus on test completion as being a major part of the Test Analyst's role. d) is not the best option as test implementation, which is a focus of the Test Analyst's role, is omitted.	TA-1.2.1 K2	1
Q2	a	a) is the correct answer. i, ii, iii, iv are objectives of the test analysis phase. Refer to the 2019 Syllabus V1.1 section 1.3. v. is an objective of test design.	TA-1.3.1 K2	1
Q3	c	c) is the correct answer. Each of the other options, while having one or more correct phrases, contain a false phrase and a false element. i. While there are advantages and disadvantages relating to independence, tests should be understandable by developers so that defects can be understood and corrected. ii. Assessors such as auditors need to understand tests as they may need to approve the tests as part of their assessment of the software conforming to standards and meeting legal regulations. iii. Communicators, such as writers of manuals, training materials or other documentation who explain the software to other stakeholders, can provide valuable input to the test design, although it is true their involvement may add delays. iv. Experienced testers may provide risk identification and system administrators may review the tests to check the system is suitable for use. The best risk identification is most likely to be achieved by calling on the broadest possible sample of stakeholders. v. Third-party partners, who are involved in the development process, should not automatically be excluded from reviewing test conditions drawn up by the company's direct employees.	TA-1.4.1 K2	1

<table>
<tr><td>Q4</td><td>c</td><td>c) is the best answer. The DAP1 specification implies there are high demands for traceability for conforming to vehicle manufacturers' specification, legal regulations and requirements of the company's finance dept. The Agile team testing DAP2 has experience in testing and previous products of this type, experience-based testing at a high-level can be effective. The other answers do not take into consideration that detailed documentation is important for DAP1. There are no arguments that support the same level of detailed documentation is required in the DAP2 part, which is a marketing project. With the experience of the Agile team on DAP2, it would take longer than necessary creating thorough documentation and Agile testing generally does not require thorough detailed documentation.</td><td>TA-1.4.2
K4</td><td>3</td></tr>
<tr><td>Q5</td><td>d</td><td>d) is the most correct answer. Option a) is not correct as low-level tests, not high-level tests, are better suited for reducing the time spent on automated test case implementation. b) is not the best option as the additional testers do not have detailed domain knowledge. c) is not the best option as high-level tests are suited to develop low-level tests and typically not vice-versa.</td><td>TA-1.4.2
K4</td><td>3</td></tr>
<tr><td>Q6</td><td>d</td><td>d) is the correct answer according to the ISTQB Syllabus, section 1.5.</td><td>TA-1.5.1
K2</td><td>1</td></tr>
<tr><td>Q7</td><td>b</td><td>b) is the correct answer. Using 1=High, 2=Medium and 3=Low, the risk assessment will rank the risks as below. In depth-first testing, all of the highest risks are run before any lower risks.
<table>
<tr><th></th><th>Task</th><th>Impact</th><th>Likelihood</th><th>Risk</th><th>Rank</th></tr>
<tr><td>A1</td><td>Add</td><td>High</td><td>High</td><td>1 x 1 = 1</td><td>= 1</td></tr>
<tr><td>A2</td><td>Add</td><td>High</td><td>Low</td><td>1 x 3 = 3</td><td>4</td></tr>
<tr><td>A3</td><td>Add</td><td>Medium</td><td>Medium</td><td>2 x 2 = 4</td><td>= 5</td></tr>
<tr><td>C1</td><td>Change</td><td>High</td><td>High</td><td>1 x 1 = 1</td><td>= 1</td></tr>
<tr><td>C2</td><td>Change</td><td>Medium</td><td>Low</td><td>2 x 3 = 6</td><td>7</td></tr>
<tr><td>C3</td><td>Change</td><td>Low</td><td>Low</td><td>3 x 3 = 9</td><td>8</td></tr>
<tr><td>D1</td><td>Delete</td><td>Medium</td><td>Medium</td><td>2 x 2 = 4</td><td>= 5</td></tr>
<tr><td>D2</td><td>Delete</td><td>High</td><td>High</td><td>1 x 1 = 1</td><td>= 1</td></tr>
</table>
</td><td>TA-2.1.1
K3</td><td>2</td></tr>
</table>

Q8	a	a) is the correct answer. Derived Equivalence Classes. Sectors flown: 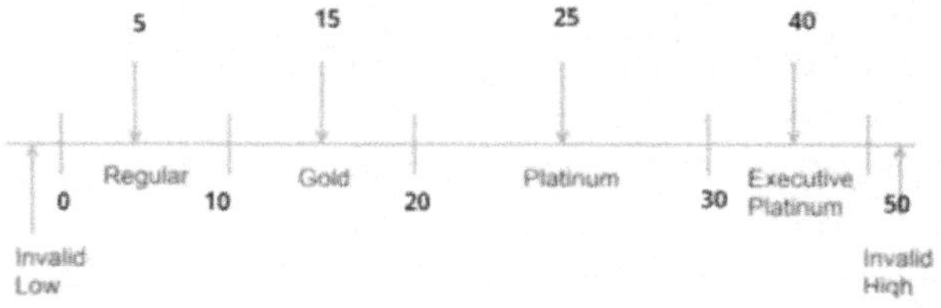 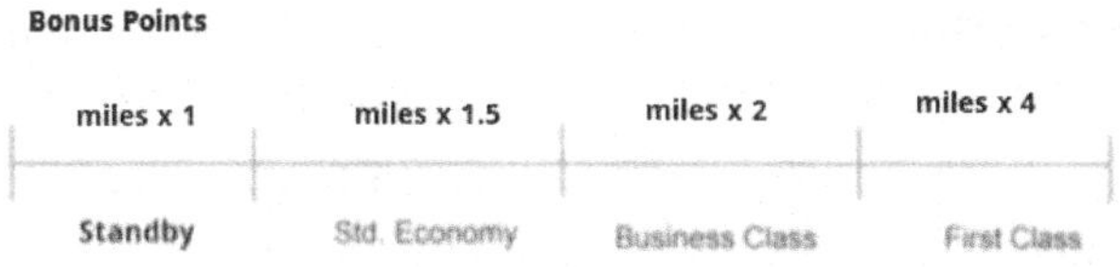 Test cases required are as below: **Sectors flown (6):** Less than 0 sectors (Invalid low) Regular ≥0 and ≤10 sectors Gold ≥11 and ≤ 19 Platinum ≥20 and <30 sectors Exec. Platinum ≥30 and <50 sectors Greater than 50 sectors (Invalid high) (Note: In practice, it may be advisable to have two tests for the partition ≥0 and ≤10 sectors (Regular) with one test for zero and one test for an integer). **Fare type (4):** Standby / Standard Economy / Business Class / First Class	TA-3.2.1 K4	3
Q9	d	d) is the correct answer. There are four partitions: 1. Up to and including -5.5°C – warning alarm 2. -5°C to 4°C – green light 3. 4.5°C to 14.5°C - yellow light 4. 15°C and over - yellow light and warning alarm (No minimum temperature below -5.5°C and no maximum above 15°C are specified, so there are no boundaries to test here) a) does not have accuracy to 0.5°C b) does not have two values -5°C boundary and also includes 0°C, which is not specified as a boundary c) Is 3-value boundary testing	TA-3.2.2 K4	3

<table>
<tr><td></td><td></td><td>Note: In practice, additional tests in partition 2 may be advisable to cover a negative number, a positive number and zero.</td><td></td><td></td></tr>
<tr><td>Q10</td><td>c</td><td>c) is the correct answer. Conditions are:
C1 Season (2): High (H), Low (L)
C2 Room Type (3): Single (S), double (D), Family (F)
C3 Weekend (2): Yes (Y), No (N)
(Christmas, New Year and Public Holidays do not need to be considered separately as they fall into the higher rates).
A full decision table is required with the number of columns equal to 12 (2 x 3 x 2) as shown below:
<table>
<tr><th>Test Case</th><th>1</th><th>2</th><th>3</th><th>4</th><th>5</th><th>6</th><th>7</th><th>8</th><th>9</th><th>10</th><th>11</th><th>12</th></tr>
<tr><td>Condition</td><td></td><td></td><td></td><td></td><td></td><td></td><td></td><td></td><td></td><td></td><td></td><td></td></tr>
<tr><td>Season</td><td>H</td><td>H</td><td>H</td><td>H</td><td>H</td><td>H</td><td>L</td><td>L</td><td>L</td><td>L</td><td>L</td><td>L</td></tr>
<tr><td>Room</td><td>S</td><td>D</td><td>F</td><td>S</td><td>D</td><td>F</td><td>S</td><td>D</td><td>F</td><td>S</td><td>D</td><td>F</td></tr>
<tr><td>Weekend</td><td>Y</td><td>N</td><td>Y</td><td>N</td><td>Y</td><td>N</td><td>Y</td><td>N</td><td>Y</td><td>N</td><td>Y</td><td>N</td></tr>
<tr><td>Action</td><td></td><td></td><td></td><td></td><td></td><td></td><td></td><td></td><td></td><td></td><td></td><td></td></tr>
<tr><td>Price</td><td>H</td><td>H</td><td>H</td><td>H</td><td>H</td><td>H</td><td>L</td><td>L</td><td>L</td><td>L</td><td>L</td><td>L</td></tr>
<tr><td>Less 15%</td><td>N</td><td>N</td><td>Y</td><td>N</td><td>N</td><td>N</td><td>N</td><td>N</td><td>N</td><td>N</td><td>N</td><td>N</td></tr>
<tr><td>Less 10%</td><td>N</td><td>N</td><td>N</td><td>N</td><td>N</td><td>N</td><td>N</td><td>N</td><td>Y</td><td>N</td><td>Y</td><td>Y</td></tr>
</table>
All columns with a single room have no discount regardless of season or day of the week so columns 1 and 4 can be collapsed to one column and 7 and 10 can be collapsed into one column. In the high season, a double room is not discounted regardless of the day of the week, so columns 2 and 5 can be collapsed to one column. In the low season, 10% discount is for a family room regardless of the day of the week, so columns 9 and 12 can be collapsed to one column. The collapsed decision table has 8 columns:
<table>
<tr><th>Test Case</th><th>1</th><th>2</th><th>3</th><th>6</th><th>7</th><th>8</th><th>9</th><th>11</th></tr>
<tr><td>Condition</td><td></td><td></td><td></td><td></td><td></td><td></td><td></td><td></td></tr>
<tr><td>Season</td><td>H</td><td>H</td><td>H</td><td>H</td><td>L</td><td>L</td><td>L</td><td>L</td></tr>
<tr><td>Room</td><td>S</td><td>D</td><td>F</td><td>F</td><td>S</td><td>D</td><td>F</td><td>D</td></tr>
<tr><td>Weekend</td><td>~</td><td>~</td><td>Y</td><td>N</td><td>~</td><td>N</td><td>~</td><td>Y</td></tr>
<tr><td>Action</td><td></td><td></td><td></td><td></td><td></td><td></td><td></td><td></td></tr>
<tr><td>Price</td><td>H</td><td>H</td><td>H</td><td>H</td><td>L</td><td>L</td><td>L</td><td>L</td></tr>
<tr><td>Less 15%</td><td>N</td><td>N</td><td>Y</td><td>N</td><td>N</td><td>N</td><td>N</td><td>N</td></tr>
<tr><td>Less 10%</td><td>N</td><td>N</td><td>N</td><td>N</td><td>N</td><td>Y</td><td>Y</td><td>N</td></tr>
</table>
</td><td>TA-3.2.3
K4</td><td>3</td></tr>
</table>

<table>
<tr>
<td></td>
<td></td>
<td>The answer can also be obtained by applying two values for conditions as specified in the Syllabus. This results in a larger table.
C1 Season: high or low?
C2 Room type: single yes/no?
C3 Room type: double yes/no?
C4 Room type: family yes/ no?
C5 Weekend: yes/no
A table is required of size 32 columns (2^5).
Collapsing the table to remove redundant and non-feasible combinations, leaves 8 columns.</td>
<td></td>
<td></td>
</tr>
<tr>
<td>Q11</td>
<td>b</td>
<td>b) is the correct answer. There are three conditions, each with two values, 'Yes' or 'No'.
C1: Paid ≤14 days?
C2: Over £500?
C3: Ordered online?
You are testing the billing component so it is not necessary to have a condition for, 'purchase made Yes/No'.
8 (2^3) columns are required for a decision table covering all combinations of conditions.
4 (2 + 2) columns are required for a decision table covering individual condition outcomes. This is from the first condition having 2 values and there being 2 additional two value conditions.
The difference is 4 (8 – 4).

Table covering all Combinations of Conditions:
<table>
<tr><th>Test Case</th><th>1</th><th>2</th><th>3</th><th>4</th><th>5</th><th>6</th><th>7</th><th>8</th></tr>
<tr><td>Condition</td><td></td><td></td><td></td><td></td><td></td><td></td><td></td><td></td></tr>
<tr><td>Paid ≤14days?</td><td>Y</td><td>Y</td><td>Y</td><td>Y</td><td>N</td><td>N</td><td>N</td><td>N</td></tr>
<tr><td>Over £500?</td><td>Y</td><td>Y</td><td>N</td><td>N</td><td>Y</td><td>Y</td><td>N</td><td>N</td></tr>
<tr><td>Ordered online?</td><td>Y</td><td>N</td><td>Y</td><td>N</td><td>Y</td><td>N</td><td>Y</td><td>N</td></tr>
<tr><td>Action</td><td></td><td></td><td></td><td></td><td></td><td></td><td></td><td></td></tr>
<tr><td>2% discount</td><td>Y</td><td>Y</td><td>Y</td><td>Y</td><td>N</td><td>N</td><td>N</td><td>N</td></tr>
<tr><td>Plus 1% discount</td><td>Y</td><td>Y</td><td>N</td><td>N</td><td>N</td><td>N</td><td>N</td><td>N</td></tr>
<tr><td>5% discount</td><td>Y</td><td>N</td><td>Y</td><td>N</td><td>Y</td><td>N</td><td>Y</td><td>N</td></tr>
<tr><td>Total % discount</td><td>8</td><td>3</td><td>7</td><td>2</td><td>5</td><td>0</td><td>5</td><td>0</td></tr>
</table>
</td>
<td>TA-3.2.3
K4</td>
<td>3</td>
</tr>
</table>

<table>
<tr>
<td></td>
<td></td>
<td>Table for Individual Condition Outcomes:
<table>
<tr><td>Test Case</td><td>1</td><td>2</td><td>3</td><td>4</td></tr>
<tr><td>Condition</td><td></td><td></td><td></td><td></td></tr>
<tr><td>Paid ≤14 days?</td><td>Y</td><td>N</td><td>Y</td><td>Y</td></tr>
<tr><td>Over £500?</td><td>Y</td><td>Y</td><td>N</td><td>Y</td></tr>
<tr><td>Ordered online?</td><td>Y</td><td>Y</td><td>Y</td><td>N</td></tr>
<tr><td>Action</td><td></td><td></td><td></td><td></td></tr>
<tr><td>2% discount</td><td>Y</td><td>N</td><td>Y</td><td>Y</td></tr>
<tr><td>Plus 1% discount</td><td>Y</td><td>N</td><td>N</td><td>Y</td></tr>
<tr><td>5% discount</td><td>Y</td><td>Y</td><td>Y</td><td>N</td></tr>
<tr><td>Total % discount</td><td>8</td><td>5</td><td>7</td><td>3</td></tr>
</table>
</td>
<td></td>
<td></td>
</tr>
<tr>
<td>Q12</td>
<td>c</td>
<td>c) is the correct answer.
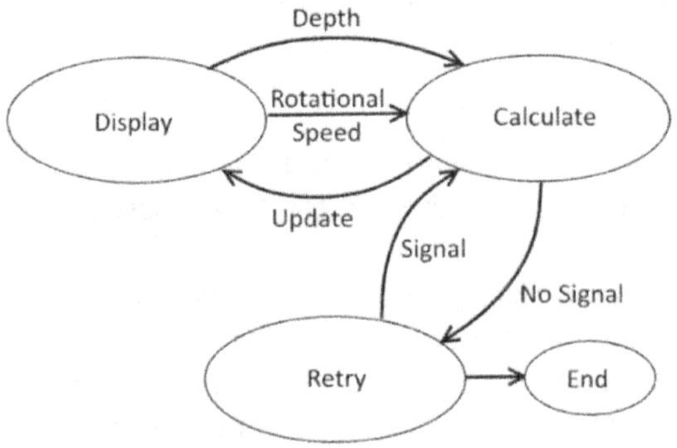

Path 1 - Display, (Depth), Calculate, (Update), Retry, Calculate, (Depth), Display [returns Depth]
Path 2 - Display, (Rotational Speed), Calculate, (Update), Display [returns Rotational Speed]
Path 3 - Display, (Rotational Speed), Calculate, (No Signal), Retry, End</td>
<td>TA-3.2.4
K4</td>
<td>3</td>
</tr>
<tr>
<td>Q13</td>
<td>b</td>
<td>b) is the correct answer. It shows both state transitions that are available from the payment requested page, one valid payment, one invalid. Option a) only shows the transition for valid. c) and d) are not correct because the question asked for transitions starting from the payment requested state.</td>
<td>TA-3.2.4
K4</td>
<td>3</td>
</tr>
</table>

<table>
<tr><td>Q14</td><td>a</td><td>a) is the correct answer. All pairs coverage will be achieved if the nine tests are run. a) Singleton coverage is also achieved because each item will be tested at least once by for example tests 1, 6 and 8 but this is not the best answer as all pairs are covered.</td><td>TA-3.2.5
K2</td><td>1</td></tr>
<tr><td>Q15</td><td>a</td><td>a) is the correct answer. There are three parameter-values for shower type (electric, mixer and thermostatic valve), five options for showerhead (hand-held only, showerhead on a slide, fixed head mounted on the wall, fixed ceiling-mounted, shower-head combined with side body jets and two options for a shower enclosure, sliding panel or folding door). Minimum number of tests equals 5 x 3 = 15. Options b) and c) are incorrect as they are below the minimum number, d) is the total number of parameter-value pairs. It is therefore correct for this scenario to assume the minimum number of tests is also equal to the actual number of tests required as no other options are given.
<table>
<tr><th>Test Case</th><th>Shower</th><th>Showerhead</th><th>Enclosure</th></tr>
<tr><td>1</td><td>Electric</td><td>Hand-held</td><td>Sliding</td></tr>
<tr><td>2</td><td>Electric</td><td>On slide</td><td>Folding</td></tr>
<tr><td>3</td><td>Electric</td><td>Fixed - wall</td><td>~</td></tr>
<tr><td>4</td><td>Electric</td><td>Fixed - ceiling</td><td>~</td></tr>
<tr><td>5</td><td>Electric</td><td>With side jets</td><td>~</td></tr>
<tr><td>6</td><td>Mixer</td><td>Hand-held</td><td>Sliding</td></tr>
<tr><td>7</td><td>Mixer</td><td>On slide</td><td>Folding</td></tr>
<tr><td>8</td><td>Mixer</td><td>Fixed - wall</td><td>~</td></tr>
<tr><td>9</td><td>Mixer</td><td>Fixed - ceiling</td><td>~</td></tr>
<tr><td>10</td><td>Mixer</td><td>With side jets</td><td>~</td></tr>
<tr><td>11</td><td>Thermostatic</td><td>Hand-held</td><td>Sliding</td></tr>
<tr><td>12</td><td>Thermostatic</td><td>On slide</td><td>Folding</td></tr>
<tr><td>13</td><td>Thermostatic</td><td>Fixed - wall</td><td>~</td></tr>
<tr><td>14</td><td>Thermostatic</td><td>Fixed - ceiling</td><td>~</td></tr>
<tr><td>15</td><td>Thermostatic</td><td>With side jets</td><td>~</td></tr>
</table></td><td>TA-3.2.6
K4</td><td>3</td></tr>
</table>

Q16	b, e	b) and e) are the untrue answers. Option a) is true. Windows 10 PC should be tested pairwise with Microsoft Edge (test case 1), Safari (test case 2) and Chrome. There is no test in the table for MS Windows 10 PC and Chrome so a) is required. b) is not true. MS Windows 10 PC is tested with Safari (test case 2) and with an external screen (test case 1). Safari and external screen are covered (test case 3) so b) is not required. c) is true. A test case is required for MS Windows / Internet Explorer and Internet Explorer /Local Screen. d) is true. A test case for Android / Safari is (as specified in the question) not required and Safari / Local is covered (test case 3) but Android / Local would not be covered if this test case was omitted so it needs the amendment. e) is not true. Chrome/External Screen would not be tested if test case 6 was omitted.	TA-3.2.6 K4	3*
Q17	d	d) is the correct answer. Additional test cases required for 100% minimum use case test coverage are: 1, 2, 3, 4, 5, E02, 6, 7, 8, E03 1, 2, 3, 4, 5, 6, 7, 8, 9, 10, 11, E04	TA-3.2.7 K4	3
Q18	d	Answer d) is the correct answer. Main path 1, 2, 3, 4, 5, 6, 7, 8, 9 Alternate path 1, 2, 3, 4, E1(2nd attempt successful), 5, E2 (no card), 9 Alternate path 1, 2, 3, 4, E1(2nd attempt fails), E1(third attempt successful), 5, E2(new card),6,7,8,9 Alternate path 1, 2, 3, 4, E1(2nd attempt), E1(third attempt fails).	TA-3.2.7 K4	3
Q19	b, c	b) and c) are the correct answers. Keep in mind the question asks for the best techniques. Option a) is not correct as there are minimal changes to the interface and the number of screen changes so it is least likely there will be a transition problem in the updated software. b) is correct. There are several inputs based on conditions that are specified and these lead to a number of actions, making a decision table a good choice. c) is correct. The new leave allocations are based on the number of years of service being in 0-10 years, 11-19 years or more than 20 years. Checking	TA-3.2.8 K4	3*

		the software correctly deals with the boundaries is a good choice. There is also the option of carrying over up to 5 days to a later year so there is a range to test here of 0-5. d) is not correct. Use case tests would emulate intended use and potentially find defects employees might encounter when using the software, but as the changes to the user interface are minimal this is not one of the best two techniques to use. e) is not correct. There are pairs, Full-time / Part-time, additional leave/no additional leave, use all leave in the year/carry forward and maternity/paternity leave /no carry forward but given the range of inputs for working out the total leave, pairwise testing is not the best option here.		
Q20	a, d	a) and d) are the correct answers. a) State transition testing is appropriate as there are a significant number of screen changes. d) Use case testing is appropriate as a key requirement is that the application must be easy and this technique emulates intended use.	TA-3.2.8 K4	3*
Q21	d, e	Answers d) and e). These options are not true because of the inclusion of 'not' in the statements.	TA-3.3.1 K2	1*
Q22	a	a) is the correct answer. Options b) and c) do not test the purchase going through to fulfilment, d) does not provide good coverage.	TA-3.3.2 K3	2
Q23	d	d) is the correct answer. The large set of existing test cases can be used as a checklist. The other options are not as appropriate.	TA-3.3.3 K2	1
Q24	a	a) is the correct answer. Option b) is not correct as the heaviest used areas may not include the functionality of a critical part of the application. In c), creating a taxonomy is not the best use of time in this scenario and targeting testing on defects does not mean all functionality is tested. d) is not the best answer here as there is no plan for the hotel to use new staff not familiar with the product and the focus should be on the software functioning as previously.	TA-3.4.1 K4	3
Q25	c	c) is the correct answer. Functional correctness, interoperability and compliance to regulations are areas specified in the scenario for special attention.	TA-4.2.1 K2	1

Q26	a	a) is the correct answer. The testing is for reasonable and meaningful text that allows the user to take appropriate action to accomplish the specified task. Functional appropriateness is usually conducted during system testing but can be conducted during the later stages of integration testing. Option b) is a functional correctness test as it is checking for what can be entered in an input field. Functional appropriateness is not conducted during component testing. c) is data verification and requires computational accuracy, so is not the best option. d) involves functional correctness of distance multiplied by mileage charge and percentage of fuel tank needing to be refilled. Functional appropriateness is not conducted during component testing.	TA-4.2.2 K2	1
Q27	d	d) is the correct answer. Option a) is not correct as the new component is correctly generating the retail price Checking the correct use of the iPad by staff is better classified as functional appropriateness. b) is not correct as functional correctness testing is required to establish both if a correct identification is made and the new component is displaying, not calculating the retail price. c) is not correct as the new component is not checking availability, functional completeness for the new component is providing the interface while amending the stock list is in the existing application.	TA-4.2.2 K2	1
Q28	d	d) is the correct answer. 1A Functional Correctness is the adherence to specified or implied requirements and can be conducted at any test level. 2D Interoperability testing focuses on the ability to exchange information and subsequently use the information that has been exchanged. 3 is best matched with B. Functional appropriateness involves evaluating and verifying the appropriateness of a set of functions for its intended task. While it is true other types of testing can be done during integration and system testing, linking the others as listed, leaves 3 to be matched with B. 4C If a requirement has not been subject to a testing process, you cannot know whether it has been completely implemented.	TA-4.2.3 K2	1

Q29	b, d	b) and d) are the two answers required. b) is not true as usability reviews are more effective when the user interface is more visible and sample screenshots are usually easier to understand and interpret than a narrative description of functionality. d) is not true as usability tests can include testing for attributes such as learnability and user interface aesthetics against usability standards documentation or reasonable outcomes.	TA-4.2.4 K2	1*
Q30	d	d) is the correct answer. Effectiveness is defined to be the capability of the test object to enable users to achieve specified goals with functional correctness and functional completeness in a specified context of use. a) and c) are incorrect. Efficiency is defined as the capability of the test object to enable users to expend appropriate amounts of resources in relation to the effectiveness achieved in a specified context of use. The options do not have details of the resources expended. For example, to calculate the time efficiency, time taken by all testers is needed. As time is not given for the tester who failed to complete the tasks, to abandon testing, time efficiency cannot be calculated. b) is incorrect. Satisfaction is defined to be the capability of the test object to satisfy users in a specified context of use. The information supplied deals with the completion of tests, it does not have information on how satisfied the users were in completing tasks, see Chapter *Measuring Usability.*	TA-4.2.4 K2	1
Q31	c	c) is the correct answer. c) is interoperability with the defect rooted in lack of correct localization for what is fast delivery (R Rapid in the UK, S Schnell in Germany) and standard delivery (S in the UK, R Regular in Germany). Option a) is not operability as the parts did not come from Germany. The likelihood is this is a local functional correctness issue. b) is a failure in the making and stocking of the part rather than a defect in the ordering software and d) is usability.	TA-4.2.5 K2	1

Q32	a	a) is the most correct answer as interactions may only be defined in system architecture and design documents. Option b) is not necessarily correct as the interaction with in-house software and the COTS product has not been tested. c) is not necessarily correct as the interaction with in-house software and the system's ability to adjust accordingly has not been tested. d) is not the best option as interoperability testing is performed during component integration and system testing.	TA-4.2.5 K2	1
Q33	a	a) is the correct answer. The Test Analyst has shared responsibility for installability and replaceability, making options b) and d) incorrect. Although limiting installation testing would save time, this is not the best approach to finding defects as they may arise in the installation of new versions, a balanced approach to the amount of testing required is better. The Test Analyst needs to repeat the installability and associated test activities after each build and not just once, so c) is not the most correct answer.	TA-4.2.6 K2	1
Q34	a, e	a) and e) are the correct answers. Although option b) could be true, it is not the best answer as adaptability tests are usually followed by functional tests. c) is not correct as adaptability, a sub-characteristic of portability is a shared responsibility between the Test Analyst and the Technical Test Analyst, d) is not the best answer as security is a different characteristic to portability which has the sub-characteristic of adaptability.	TA-4.2.7 K4	3*
Q35	c	c) is the correct answer. Both buttons 'Proceed' and 'Delete' will result in the database being erased. The second button should be 'Cancel'.	TA-4.2.7 K4	3

Q36	d	d) is the correct option. i. is not respected as there are two R2020-123 requirements, so the identifiers are not unique. ii. is respected as the style guide does have a version number. iii. is not respected. The use of 'width' is used in the first requirement and in the R2020-126 'base' is used. This makes it unclear if the width of the FM5NE logo is to be altered and then the height to keep consistency as specified in the first requirement. Also, the requirements refer to 'articles received on client cases' and 'published content items which may come from clients.' It is not clear if these are the same or different. iv. is respected. The requirements contain adequate detail to be testable. v. is respected. The requirements are from the identified marketing document.	TA-5.2.1 K3	2
Q37	c	c) is the correct answer. A tight schedule is stated in the question, but the story has no specific priority.	TA-5.2.2 K3	2
Q38	a, b	a) and b) are the correct answers. Option a) is not met as there is no priority. b) is not met. There are dependencies on other components being software available could make this testing this not viable. D2 refers to the purchasing component. The user story could use a driver but that is not stated. D3 and D5 deal with membership criteria and there is no information suggesting membership software is included in the component under test. c) is met. The outcomes are testable. d) is met. 'Who' is a new user, 'what' is use the Frequent Flyer program, 'why' is to access the benefits of the program. e) is met. The story is written from the view of the user.	TA-5.2.2 K3	2*
Q39	d	d) is the correct answer. A previous step may have produced incorrect data but the problem doesn't surface until later in this scenario, as a Test Analyst you have responsibility for initially analysing failures, making option a) not correct. b) and c) do not address the problem of a failure.	TA-6.2.1 K3	2

Q40	a	a) is the correct answer. b) is not the best option as it is incorrect to assume tools can automate all manual tests. Not all test results are machine-interpretable and therefore cannot be automated. c) is not correct. The Test Analyst does not necessarily know underlying low-level programming, high-level would allow the Test Analyst to write tests in 'human' language. d) is not correct as the return on investment for automated execution tools is usually highest when using automation regression tests because of low-level maintenance, expected and repeated execution.	TA-6.3.1 K2	1

* If both options selected are correct, the full number of points assigned to the question are awarded, otherwise no points are given.

PREPARE FOR PRACTICE EXAM TWO

Well done for completing Practice Exam One
Improve your marks still further.

Before Attempting Practice Exam Two
Review your results from Practice Exam One. Make a review list of the questions where you did not get the correct answer. Also, make a review list of questions where you had correct answers but feel that you achieved this by guesswork.

Review your lists with reference to not knowing or incorrectly knowing a term. Learn the definition of terms you are unsure of.

Review your lists with reference to not spotting a negative word, such as a question asking for which is an untrue or incorrect answer. If you missed this, make a point of looking for negative words in Practice Exam Two.

Review your lists with reference to having chosen the wrong option because of a word or small phrase embedded in the question which affects the answer, see Chapter *About the Exam - How to Approach Exam Questions.* Add your entries to those listed in the chapter.

For each of the questions on your review lists, look up the Learning Objective, see Chapter *Practice Exam One Answers - Answer grid.* For some Learning Objectives, there is one question, for others there are two questions. Where two questions are indicated against the Learning Objective for a question you have had difficulty with, check if, in Practice Exam One, you answered the second question correctly. Work on increasing your knowledge in the areas indicated by the Learning Objectives, use the Syllabus, read relevant parts of this book and other reliable sources.

Look at the Knowledge levels of the questions on your review lists, see Chapter *Practice Exam One Answers - Answer grid*. While keeping in mind the distribution of questions, (see Chapter *About the Exam – Where Marks can be Gained or Lost)* identify where your skill gaps are, K2 Understand, K3 Apply or K4 Analyze. Work on your skills appropriately. If you need more marks from K2 questions, learn more details and commit more to memory. Make a list of terms you were not confident with. Revise these using the Glossary. If you need more practice on K3 and K4, go back to studying examples in this book and look for scenarios from your work or other sources.

Consider the time taken to answer questions, including those answered correctly. Details on the suggested time for a question is based on the K-level, see Chapter *Knowledge Levels and Learning Objectives – Knowledge Levels.* If you feel that a few questions took significantly longer than the time suggested, review why this happened and aim to improve on your knowledge and skills as appropriate.

The exam is specified with mandatory questions on all the Learning Objectives being included, except for question 6. This question is a selectable question and can be based on one of the three Learning Objectives, TA-1.4.3, TA-1.5.1 and TA-1.6.1. In Practice Exam One, question #6 is based on TA-1.5.1. To check your knowledge of the other two Learning Objectives, try the following questions.

Exam Selectable Questions

Question #6a TA-1.4.3 (1 Point)

You are testing a new website that allows users to enrol online for deliveries of study materials. The requirements document is detailed and includes requirement R102, the user is allowed up to three attempts to log in.

Test Case ID: 2020-1. (R102)
Title: Log in to the website
Description: Up to three attempts are allowed for logging in
Assumptions: User has a supported device and browser
Post-conditions: User is logged in
Test steps with a state-transition table:

1. Open website
2. Enter the username and password in the appropriate fields
3. Click 'Login'
4. Continue as laid out in the state transition table

State	Login	Correct Password	Incorrect Password
S1	First Attempt	S4	S2
S2	Second Attempt	S4	S3
S3	Third Attempt	S4	S5
S4	User Page		

Which two of the following are required but have not been included?

a) Preconditions are adequately defined
b) Expected results have explicit pass/fail criteria
c) Test design is objective
d) Traceability back to the test basis is included
e) Post-condition for the expected successful result is clear

Select TWO options

Question #6b TA-1.6.1 (1 Point)

Test execution can include the following tasks:

i. Executing manual tests, including exploratory testing
ii. Making suggestions for future exploratory testing sessions based on the findings from exploratory testing
iii. Analyzing anomalies to establish their likely causes
iv. Recognizing defect clusters which may indicate the need for more testing of a particular part of the test object
v. Making suggestions for improving any of the work products from the test implementation activity (e.g. improvements to test procedures)

According to the ISTQB Syllabus, which of the following is correct?

a) i, ii, iii, iv are tasks which may be conducted by either the tester or the Test Analyst, v is a typical additional task which may be performed by the Test Analyst
b) ii, iii, v are tasks which may be conducted by either the tester or the Test Analyst, i, iv are typical additional tasks which may be performed by the Test Analyst
c) i, iv, v are tasks which may be conducted by either the tester or the Test Analyst, ii, iii are typical additional tasks which may be performed by the Test Analyst
d) i, iii are tasks which may be conducted by either the tester or the Test Analyst, ii, iv and v are typical additional tasks which may be performed by the Test Analyst

Select ONE option

Answers to Exam Selectable Questions

Question	Correct Answer	Explanation / Rationale	Learning Objective (LO) / K-Level	Points
Q6a	a, b	a) and b) are the answers required. a) is not included. No explicit conditions state the user must have a valid username, password and account. b) is not included. The result S5 for a failed third attempt is not documented. c) is included. The test case is observable and has a measurable objective of test execution. d) Traceability is included in the test case ID. e) Post-condition for the expected successful result is the user will be logged in.	TA-1.4.3 K2	1*
Q6b	d	d) is the correct answer. See ISTQB Syllabus 2019 V1.1 section 1.6 – Test Execution for lists of the tasks conducted by either the tester or the Test Analyst and the list of additional tasks.	TA-1.6.1 K2	1

* If both options selected are correct, the full number of points assigned to the question are awarded, otherwise no points are given.

PRACTICE EXAM TWO QUESTIONS

40 Questions – 2019 Syllabus
Time allowed 120 minutes
52 / 80 marks are required for a Pass

Question #1 (1 Point)

The amount of involvement, time required, information available and expectations for testing can vary with different Software Development Life Cycle (SDLC) models. For Agile projects, consider the following:

i. When compared to other life cycle models, the earliest involvement from the Test Analyst is required
ii. High-level planning is undertaken for each iteration
iii. It is common to have a much closer working relationship with stakeholders than might be the case with other life cycle models
iv. Closure tasks are done at the end of each iteration
v. Reviews are continuous as the software evolves

Which of the above statements are true?

a) i, ii, iv
b) i, iii, v
c) ii, iv, v
d) iii, iv, v

Select ONE option

Question #2 (1 Point)

As a Test Analyst, you are working on an update to a ticketing application. The application has been in production for three years and there is documentation from that time. The update must have all the existing functionality as well as new features. The new features have been specified in the requirements specification which has passed review with reasonable results. Tasks include:

i. Use of the requirements specification to identify test conditions
ii. Talking to relevant stakeholders during a workshop to identify test conditions
iii. Identifying prioritization criteria
iv. Determining the design techniques to be used
v. Identifying any required infrastructure including tools

Which tasks above should the Test Analyst undertake or contribute to during test analysis?

a) i, ii, iii
b) i, iii, v
c) ii, iii, iv
d) i, iv, v

Select ONE option

Question #3 (1 Point)

Stakeholders can provide useful knowledge and expertise to a project.

Which the following are most true?

a) Having a large number of stakeholders is always beneficial for a project
b) Stakeholders can provide input that uncovers and reduces risks
c) Input from Stakeholders does not alter project requirements and constraints
d) Stakeholders can affect the granting of acceptance of the project
e) Stakeholders' expectations for the project will be realistic

Select TWO options

Question #4 (3 Points)

You are working on an update to an application that tracks delivery trucks for a company which has a central depot and transports shipping crates to ports for onward delivery. The application must comply with the latest Freight Transport Association's regulations. GPS location data input is used and should this fail, due to an unspecified reason such as poor weather, obstruction of the signal by a building or being in a tunnel, the application should continue with estimated positions until GPS location data is restored. The company plans to introduce automated testing for future updates. Requirements for this update are specified in full, a summary of some of these is below:

i. R2020-1 Improved calculation of the estimated position when GPS data input fails, using the specified method of calculation
ii. R2020-2 New display of geofenced areas and dead zones. These areas may be transient and subject to change
iii. R2020-3 Improved fleet administration with the online map display to include specified vehicle symbols and colour status (moving, parked, idle) that stand out against the map background
iv. R2020-4 Monitoring of fuel usage with size of engine, weight of truck and distance travelled to allow for comparisons with existing data
v. R2020-4 Truck drivers must not work without a break more than current regulations allow

Base on the information above, which is the best approach to take?

a) Low-level tests for all update requirements
b) Low-level tests for i and ii, high-level test for iii, iv, v
c) Low-level tests for i, iii, iv, v high-level test for ii
d) Low-level tests for iii and iv, high-level tests for i, ii and v

Select ONE option

Question #5 (3 Points)

You are testing a funds transfer application for a large multi-national bank. Up to 50,000 transactions are processed in any day. The requirements specification is clear, detailed and exhaustive. Automation of testing is planned for the future. The transactions, often made between currencies, may involve rounding and must be accurate to 8 decimal places. The testers are domain experts without specific formal testing experience. Independent verification of tests is required for auditing purposes.

With the information given above, which of the following statements is most correct?

a) High-level test cases should be used as testers are domain experts
b) High-level test cases should be used as these do not limit tester ingenuity and provide a better basis for future automation of test cases
c) High-level test cases should be used as these are better suited to re-use in different test cycles when different data can be used and the test cases can be used in audit verification. Traceability will be achieved by using test case naming conventions
d) Low-level test cases should be used with detailed test procedures and documentation. Traceability from the low-level test cases to the requirements should be also assured

Select ONE option

Question #6 (1 Point)

You are reviewing the test log below to determine what actions are required:

Test	Expected Result	Actual Result	Outcome
1	Valid account entered	Valid account	Pass
2	120 loyalty points	100 loyalty points	Pass
3	Voucher for £5	Voucher for £5	Pass
4	10% discount on total	1% discount on total	Fail
5	Switch to information on delivery options	Sent to 'Checkout' where there are tick boxes for delivery	Fail

On further investigation, test 4 was resolved as a typographical error in the log and the actual result was 10% as expected.

Which of the following options represents the best action to take next?

a) Repeat tests 2, 4, and 5. Raise incident reports if these tests produce the same results. As executing more tests may result in a delay in reporting test results, inform the Test Manager of what has happened.

b) Raise an incident report for test 5. Check test documentation for test 2 and raise an incident report if the expected result and actual result are both correct. Update the log entry for 2 to indicate 'Fail'. Repeat test 4 without running test 3 first to establish if the problem with the outcome of test 4 arose as a result of executing test 3 immediately beforehand.

c) Check specification documentation for the expected outcomes for tests 2 and 4 and compare this with log entries. If this doesn't resolve the discrepancies, raise incident reports. If it does resolve the discrepancies, update the log entries for 2 and 4.

d) Check specification documentation for the expected outcomes for tests 2 and 5 and compare with the log entries. If this does not resolve the discrepancies, raise incident reports. If it does resolve the discrepancies, update the log entries for tests 2 and 5 to show similar correct expected and actual results and update the entries for 4 and 5 to pass.

Select ONE option

Question #7 (2 Points)

You are testing the third revision of an application, due to be deployed to replace the version in production. You have the following documents available at the appropriate stages during the project:

1. Report from the previous two versions, detailing defects that were found and assessments of the likelihood of the defects occurring
2. Report on defects discovered so far during test execution, which sub-system these defects occurred in, and an assessment of their severity, with re-evaluation of defects where additional information has become known
3. Checklist of important quality characteristics for the application under test with input from the broadest possible sample of stakeholders and testers who have experience to translate the test conditions into test cases
4. Report on usability testing based on a prototype in which both the impact and the likelihood of defects occurring have been determined

As a Test Analyst, you are actively involved in the following risk-based tasks:

A. Risk identification
B. Prioritisation
C. Risk assessment
D. Risk mitigation

Which of the following is the most appropriate categorisation for the documents listed above?

a) 1C, 2D, 3A, 4B
b) 1A, 2B, 3C, 4D
c) 1C, 2A, 3D, 4B
d) 1B, 2C, 3A, 4D

Select ONE option

Question #8 (3 Points)

You are testing an application for collecting Stamp Duty Land Tax (SDLT) on the purchase of properties in the United Kingdom. Various percentages of tax apply depending on the purchase price. A purchase price of less than £1 should return an error. The tax is calculated using the bands below:

Band	Rate Percentage
Up to £125,000	0%
£125,001 to £250,000	2%
£250,001 to £925,000	5%
£925,001 to £1.5m	10%
Above £1.5m	12%

For example, when buying a £275,000 property, SDLT is calculated, 0% on the first £125,000 = £0, 2% on the next £125,000 = £2,500, 5% on the final £25,000 = £1,250, Total SDLT = £3,750.

Using equivalence partitioning, which set of tests is the least number to give 100% coverage?

a) £0, £1, £125k, £250k, £925k, £1.5m
b) £0, £1, £100k, £300k, £500k, £1m, £2m
c) £1, £200k, £300k, £1m, £2m
d) None of the above

Select ONE option

Question #9 (3 Points)

You are a Test Analyst working on an application for a company that runs a fitness gym and swimming pool. The company provides incentives to customers based on the number of sessions bought in the previous twelve months. Customers are given a discount on the annual membership charge. Sessions can be either gym or swimming or a mix of both.

1-12	Sessions	5% discount
13-24	Sessions	10% discount
Over 24	Sessions	15% discount

The maximum number of sessions is specified each year depending on previous usage of the centre.

Using two value boundary testing, which of the following is the correct set of tests to achieve 100% coverage with the minimum number of cases?

a) 0, 1, 12, 25, max sessions
b) 1, 12, 13, 24, 25, max sessions, max sessions plus 1
c) 0, 1, 11, 12, 23, 24, 25, max sessions, max sessions plus 2 (1 swimming, 1 gym)
d) 0, 1, 12, 13, 24, 25, max sessions, max sessions plus 1

Select ONE option

Question #10 (3 Points)

You are testing an application for a University. A student wishing to take the end of course exam should have a minimum of 80% attendance of the lectures. Also, the student must have gained 5 or more marks out of 10 for three coursework essays or 8 or more marks for two coursework essays. If the student has previously taken an exam at this level in another faculty, there is no requirement to meet the attendance criteria. You are considering using either a decision table covering all combinations of conditions for feasible and non-redundant combinations or a decision table covering all individual condition outcomes where all values are initially set to 'True'.

How many more test cases are required for testing all combinations of feasible and non-redundant conditions above the number for testing all individual condition outcomes?

a) 0
b) 1
c) 2
d) 8

Select ONE option

Question #11 (3 Points)

An events company is staging a new exhibition, running for four weeks. Tickets can be bought online. The ticket prices are as follows:

Ticket Type	Price in GBP
Adult (A)	£20
Student (S)	£10
Child (C)	£6

To promote the exhibition, the company has issued 1,000 promotion codes giving £1 off the ticket price for the first two weeks. Furthermore, for visitors on Mondays, there is a 50% discount which is applied to the original ticket price and then is additive to the promotion code if it is presented during the first two weeks of the exhibition.

Using decision table testing, how many test cases are required to cover all non-redundant and feasible decision rules?

a) 12 for the first two weeks, 6 for the last two weeks
b) 16 for the first two weeks, 12 for the last two weeks
c) 9 for the first two weeks, 6 for the last two weeks
d) 16 for the first two weeks, 9 for the last two weeks

Select ONE option

Question #12 (3 Points)

A car owner submits a payment claim to his car insurance company. This claim follows the sequence shown in the diagram. If information is missing, the claim can be moved back from 'Activate' to 'Acceptance'. If new information changes while in the 'Activate' state the claim is reactivated. If a claim is disputed, it can only be returned to the state from which it came.

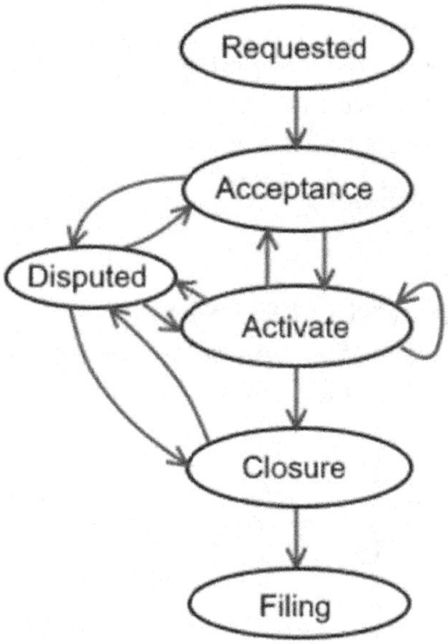

From 'Activate', how many valid 1-switch transitions are there?

a) 4
b) 5
c) 7
d) 9

Select ONE Option

Question #13 (3 Points)

As a Test Analyst, you have been asked to look into a reported problem occurring with a banking application that allows users to set up savings accounts online. When a user checks her current account, goes to set up a new savings account and then transfers money from her current account into the savings account, the transaction is successful. However, if the user first sets up the savings account and then checks the balance in her current account, transferring money into the savings account is unsuccessful.

Using state transition testing, which level should you most focus on for this type of problem?

a) 0-switch
b) 1-switch
c) 2-switch
d) Round-trip

Select ONE option

Question #14 (1 Point)
Which test design technique is often used to determine values for the nodes of the classification tree?

a) Use cases
b) Equivalence partitioning
c) Decision tables
d) None of the above

Select ONE option

Question #15 (3 Points)
The classification tree below shows four test cases. No dependencies are specified. All parameter-values are included in the four cases.

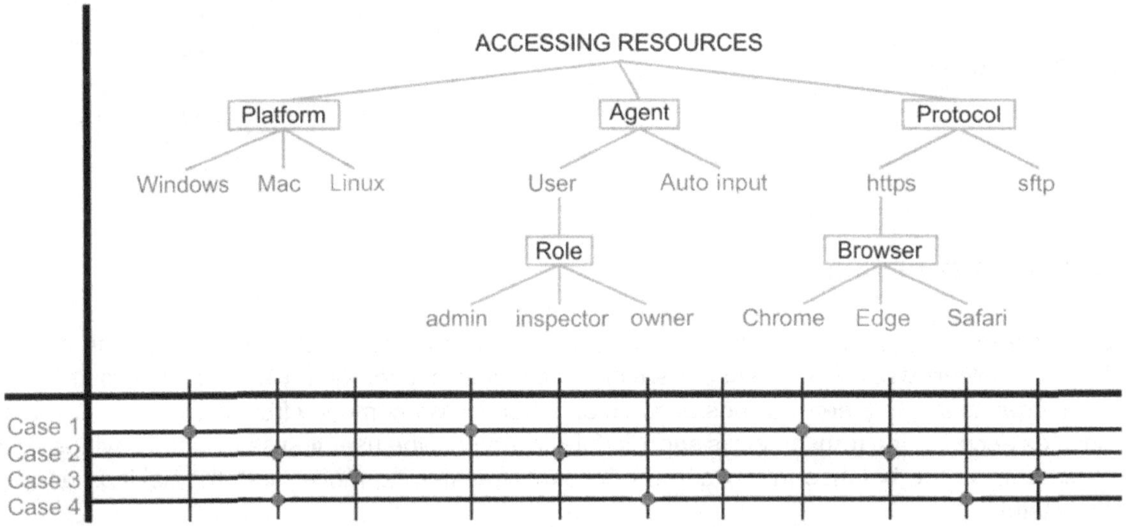

Using pairwise testing for this scenario, how many test cases are required for 100% testing of all parameters and parameter-value pairs?

a) 4
b) 8
c) 16
d) 40

Select ONE option

Question #16 (3 Points)

You are working for a company about to launch a new computer. The computer comes with either an SSD or HDD disc drive. The customer can specify a standard or extended keyboard, the latter having numbers on the right-hand side of the keyboard. For gaming use, the company recommends an NVIDIA® graphics card, alternatively the computer can be configured with an AMD® graphics card. The customer can choose between a standard 20-inch screen or an external 27-inch screen.

It has been decided that pairwise testing with 100% coverage is required. How many test cases are needed?

a) 6
b) 16
c) 4
d) 24

Select ONE option

Question #17 (3 Points)

As a Test Analyst, you have been brought in to help with testing an application that allows a user to select a wash-basin online. You are reviewing the use case below:

USE CASE: Wash-basin with plug. Use case ID: UC-1717
Purpose: Select wash-basin
Actors: Returning user, new user, wash-basin selection software
Preconditions: None. Post-condition: Exit with data to 'Purchase goods'

Main Scenario:

1. User logs in
   - 1.1 User is new and decides to create an account
   - 1.2 User creates an account and is returned to login
2. System prompts 'pedestal' or 'wall-mounted' basin
3. User selects 'wall-mounted'
4. System prompts 'standard taps' or 'customized taps'
5. User selects 'standard taps'
   - 5.1 User is taken to 'customisation' for customized tap fittings and selection data is then passed back
   - 5.2 Use case continues
6. System prompts 'plug with attached chain?'
   - 6.1 User selects 'No chain' option
   - 6.2 System prompts 'Flip-up' or 'Pop-up' plug option
   - 6.3 User selects 'Flip-up'
     - 6.3.1 System confirms 'Pop-up' and continues at 6.5
   - 6.4 System confirms choice of 'Flip-up'
   - 6.5 System identifies wash-basins that cannot accommodate choice of plug and removes these from the list of possible wash-basins
7. System displays possible wash-basins meeting the user's selected options
8. User confirms selection

Test case one: 1, 2, 3, 4, 5, 6, 7, 8
Test case two: 1, 1.1, 1.2, 2, 3, 4, 5, 5.1, 5.2, 6, 6.1, 6.2, 6.3, 6.4, 7, 8

Which of the following statements are most true?

a) Using two test cases may mean defects are masked
b) Two test cases provide the minimum coverage required
c) Use case main path emulates the intended use of the system
d) Alternate paths are fully covered
e) Use case does not provide coverage of all of the application requirements

Select TWO options

Question #18 (3 Points)

As a Test Analyst, you are working on an application for online purchases of spare parts. You have received the following use case:

USE CASE: Online order — Use Case ID: UC-1818
Purpose: Purchase item — Actors: User, software
Preconditions: User has a supported device and browser
Post-conditions: Invoice (paid) and tracking number

User	System
1. User logs into an account	2. System verifies valid account (E1)
3. User searches for item	4. System confirms available stock and price (E2)
5. User confirms selection	6. System displays previously stored billing and delivery address(es)
7. User confirms displayed billing and delivery address(es) (E3)	8. System provides total cost of the order, price of the item(s), VAT tax if applicable and delivery charges
9. User confirms order and acceptance of cost (E4)	10. System requests payment method
11. User indicates payment method by entering card PIN details (E4)	12. System validates payment card and PIN (E5)
	13. System processes payment, indicates order successfully placed and provides invoice (paid) and tracking number
14. User exits	

E1 User is asked to set up an account with billing and delivery information, log in to the account and use case continues
E2 System reports no availability of the item, asks user if she wants to return to step 3 or user exit and takes appropriate action depending on the user's response
E3 User enters new or amended billing and delivery details. System validates these and use case continues
E4 User decides to abandon order. System confirms order has been cancelled and offers user the choice of returning to step 3 or alternately to user exit
E5 Payment problem, system asks user to re-enter payment details (one additional attempt allowed) and then use case continues. On subsequent payment problem, system takes user to user exit.

How many test cases are required to achieve 100% minimum test coverage for this use case?

a) 2
b) 4
c) 5
d) 6

Select ONE option

Question #19 (3 Points)

As a Test Analyst, you are working on an application for a large distribution company which sends goods to customer locations worldwide. You have been asked to review the application's handling of costs associated with weight. Up to 5,000 packages are sent out each day. The shipping cost is dependent on where the weight of the goods fits in a set range of predetermined rates, the size meets certain criteria and the destination (UK, Europe or other countries).

Which of the following techniques would be the most useful?

a) Classification trees
b) Boundary value analysis
c) Decision tables
d) Equivalence partitions

Select ONE option

Question #20 (3 Points)

As a Test Analyst, you have been brought in to work on an update to an application used by a bathroom tile supplier. The existing application provides a visual model of the customer's bathroom with choice of wall tiles and the number of tiles required. The tiles can be square or rectangular, large, medium or small. The company now wishes to provide customers with a visual model that optionally includes specified wall coverings. The new options include wall-mounted mirrors of specified sizes, shower wallboards and wall-mounted cupboards. The specification includes detailed information about the number of tiles that should be removed when a particular option is added. To meet the required delivery time, the existing application is being used as the basis for the update, so the required functionality can be generated more quickly than working from scratch.

Which of the following test techniques would together be the best approach to take within the available time frame?

a) Experience-based techniques
b) Classification tree
c) Boundary value analysis
d) Use case testing
e) Equivalence partitioning

Select TWO options

Question #21 (1 Point)

As a Test Analyst, you are working on a localisation project with an application that provides travel information for visas and other requirements for entering a country as well as a currency exchange calculator. There have been issues with usability and the user interface. Travellers starting journeys in the United Kingdom and also originating from several other countries use the application. You have decided to use error guessing with a taxonomy. You need to select a user interface taxonomy.

Which of the following are the most appropriate to be included in the taxonomy?

a) Entry fields should support characters required in the target language with sub-categories for each specific language character set
b) Time and date fields for inputting time of travel should be formatted for the target language with sub-categories for the different order, such as US month/day/year and UK day/month/year
c) Response times for completing similar tasks should be approximately the same regardless of the country where the traveller might be
d) Currency exchange with sub-categories for correct calculation and exchange rate should be used
e) Data should be accurately stored with a sub-category of lists sorted alphabetically according to local language spelling

Select TWO options

Question #22 (2 Points)

You are a Test Analyst working on a new e-commerce project. The high-level requirements documents have few details and the timescale for the project is tight. You have been brought in to conduct exploratory testing.

Which of the following statements about exploratory testing are not true?

a) Good exploratory testing is pro-active and unplanned as it uses the tester's experience
b) The Test Manager may choose to hold a debriefing session to gather the results
c) To be of use, automation tools must have capture/playback capability, record the steps taken by the exploratory tester and record the expected outcomes
d) A test charter can be used to identify what is in scope and what is out of scope
e) Defects that fall between functional boundaries may be found

Select TWO options

Question #23 (1 Point)
Which of the following statements is most often untrue for effective defect-based testing?

a) Does not reference the requirements specification to derive tests
b) Allows the tester to target a specific type of defect
c) Helps to leverage industry-standard knowledge to derive particular tests
d) Does not use lists of identified risks and risk scenarios as a basis for targeting tests

Select ONE option

Question #24 (3 Points)
You are testing an application for a grocery store that offers incentives, dependent on the size of order, to customers holding loyalty cards. Wine and beer are excluded from incentives. There have been several documented defects where some customers have been given a higher discount level than the one they are entitled to. You suspect these may be due to some loyalty cards having expired but still allowing incentives, rounding errors on payment thresholds or non-qualifying goods being included erroneously.

Which of the following would be the best techniques to use in this situation?

a) Boundary value analysis
b) Decision tables
c) Equivalence partitioning
d) Error guessing
e) Defect-taxonomy tests

Select TWO options

Question #25 (1 Point)

As a Test Analyst, you are working on a project testing an updated application that handles peer-to-peer lending transactions for banking customers. The application must have good usability. Much of the code handling loan calculations and account payments is being re-used from the previous version of the application, which has been in use since its initial market release two years ago. Several new functions are being added to enhance the user experience and improve the display of graphical information. Users have had very little involvement in the definition of the new features and design aspects. The features have been implemented according to the developer's preferences. There is a tight schedule for the testing.

Which of the following quality characteristics would you focus on most during testing?

a) Functional correctness
b) Compatibility
c) Functional appropriateness
d) Functional completeness

Select ONE option

Question #26 (1 Point)

Which is the most correct statement?

a) Functional correctness testing is performed to evaluate and validate the ability of the system to carry out the requirements needed for specified usage objectives
b) Functional appropriateness testing verifies the application's adherence to the specified or implied requirements and may give indications that the system will not be able to meet the needs of the user in an acceptable way
c) Functional completeness testing is performed to determine the coverage of specified tasks and user objectives by the implemented functionality. Lower than expected levels of functional completeness are indications that the system has not been fully implemented
d) Functional completeness testing involves evaluating and validating a set of functions for its intended use and may give indications that the system will not be able to meet the needs of the user in an acceptable way

Select ONE option

Question #27 (1 Point)

You are working on an update to an application used by a travel company. As part of the holiday travel package, users can book taxis to the airport for their flights. The user enters the flight time, number of passengers, luggage requirements and pick up location. When using the previous version of the application, users have not always arrived with sufficient time to check-in and purchase gifts. Some flights have been missed. The travel company has been receiving higher than expected charges from the taxi operators. Problems have arisen when taxis have taken longer routes or have been delayed due to heavy traffic, road closures or having to avoid low emission zones. In the updated application, the time allowed to reach the airport is increased by 10% and for peak times by an additional 15%.

You have the following for test cases:

Test case 1: With 10% extra time, an old type taxi with a pick-up from a location where the route to the airport must avoid a low-emissions zone, will arrive in time
Test case 2: Accuracy in adding 10% additional time
Test case 3: Accuracy in adding 15% additional time where appropriate
Test case 4: Fare charged to the travel company

Which of the options below best describe the test cases above?

a) 1, 2 and 4 are functional correctness 3 is functional appropriateness
b) 1 and 2 are functional correctness, 3 and 4 are functional appropriateness
c) 2, 3 and 4 are functional correctness, 1 is functional appropriateness
d) 3 and 4 are functional correctness, 1 and 2 are functional appropriateness

Select ONE option

Question #28 (1 Point)

As a Test Analyst, you have been assigned to a project developing an application for a car Insurance company. Users can log in using iPads, PCs with Microsoft Windows™ 10, mobile devices running iOS 13, Android 9 or later versions. The application will calculate expected premiums, based on the model of motor vehicle, engine size, vehicle age, driver's accident record and driver's age. The user can request fully comprehensive or basic third-party only cover. The user is then provided with a summary and indicative price for submission to the company's call-centre staff for verification or amendment, confirmation and, if the user accepts the insurance, purchase completion. The application must also produce reports on the number of policies requested and the number sold for the management team. The following is an extract from the agreed testing plan:

1. During integration testing, testing must be conducted for all specified factors that influence the premium price
2. During integration testing, testing accident records must be checked on the external central register of accidents and, if required, amendments to the premium made as specified in the documentation
3. During system testing, tests must be conducted for checking the application fulfils the requirements of all intended users, those having different motor vehicles, different ages and different accident records
4. During system testing, testing must be conducted to check the software covers the specified user objective of providing a summary of cover, indicative price and confirmation of the sale if appropriate

The tests can be categorised as follows:

A. Functional correctness
B. Functional appropriateness
C. Interoperability
D. Functional completeness

Which of the following is most correct for categorizing the tests?

a) 1A, 2C, 3D, 4B
b) 1B, 2C, 3D, 4A
c) 1A, 2C, 3B, 4D
d) 1C, 2D, 3B, 4A

Select ONE option

Question #29 (1 Point)

Which two of the following statements best explain aspects of functional appropriateness testing?

a) Usually conducted during system testing or later stages of integration
b) Covers tests for the necessary steps to complete tasks and excludes unnecessary steps
c) Can be based on decision tables or use cases
d) Verifies adherence to the specified or implied requirements
e) A lower than expected level of functional appropriateness indicates the system has not been fully implemented

Select TWO options

Question #30 (1 Point)

As a Test Analyst, you are working an updated application for real estate agents to list online properties for sale. There were very few usability requirements previously documented but it was thought that the user interface was dull. The updated user interface has been improved, new features added and the time to load property details is reduced. You have been brought onto the project as it has been noticed that there have been fewer uptakes by new users than expected. You have experience in testing but not with this particular product. The product is stable and summative usability testing has been completed.

To assess usability, which of the following would be the best action to take?

a) Verify all stated usability requirements have been met and validate usability by conducting usability testing in a lab with a sample of the experienced users
b) Verify all stated usability requirements have been met and validate usability by conducting usability testing in a lab with a sample of prospective users
c) Verify usability using experience-based testing and validate usability by conducting usability testing in a lab with a sample of a range of inexperienced users
d) Verify usability by conducting formative usability testing and validate usability by simulating a realistic load in the lab environment and verifying the user experience with the response time

Select ONE option

Question #31 (1 Point)

Interoperability testing is a responsibility of the Test Analyst. Consider the following:

i. The exchange of information between two or more components
ii. The exchange of information between two or more systems
iii. The application or system can function correctly in all intended target environments
iv. An application based on the Internet of Things behaves as expected
v. The application can be deployed into its intended environment

Interoperability testing should be performed to verify which of the above?

a) i, ii, iii, v
b) ii, iii
c) i, ii, iv
d) i, iv, v

Select ONE option

Question #32 (1 Point)

You are working on an application that allows several companies within a business group to communicate with external suppliers to satisfy customer orders. Requests may be synchronous or asynchronous. A product may be in stock, unavailable due to an incorrect product code having been requested, on backorder or out of stock due to discontinuation of the product line. The requirements specify 'product not available' applies to 'out of stock' due to discontinuation of the product line. Other messages are to be used in other circumstances. The account may be put on 'hold' if there is an outstanding payment over an agreed amount, the order exceeds the credit allowed or a higher number of items than permitted from one product line have been requested. The rules and thresholds for putting a 'hold' on an account vary between the different suppliers. The requirements specify the reason for the 'hold' should be returned and displayed to the company making the request.

Using the information above, during interoperability testing, which two of the following are the best actions for the Test Analyst to take?

a) Verify the updated application can be installed on the companies' systems
b) Conduct Test cases where the timing of the request/response can be altered
c) Conduct test cases to process handling of a response 'product not available'
d) There is no need to have test cases for the different reasons for putting a stop on an account as these are different depending on the supplier
e) Check response times from each of the external suppliers to look up availability of the product(s) is consistent

Select TWO options

Question #33 (1 Point)

Which of the following are examples of where portability testing would be required?

i. Software designed to be used with Microsoft Edge® browser and Google Chrome browser
ii. Software designed to be used with Microsoft SQL server® and Oracle® databases
iii. Installation of software on Microsoft Windows 10 and Windows XP operating systems
iv. Uninstallation of software on macOS® and Linux operating systems
v. Systems based on the Internet of Things (IoT)

a) iii, iv, v
b) i, ii, v
c) i, ii, iii, iv
d) i, ii, v

Select ONE option

Question #34 (3 Points)

You are a Test Analyst working on a new application for an electricity distribution company. The company draws power from nuclear power stations, gas-fired stations and wind turbine sources in amounts dependent on demand. Maximum use is to be made of wind-generated renewable energy.

The requirements include:

a) Wind weather data is processed in real-time and the application selects the maximum amount of power that can be delivered by wind generators
b) Electricity transmission is via the shortest network route. Should that route fail, for example due to poor weather, an alternative routing is used
c) Power distributed within the system is tracked at all times and used to compute the total power. This is communicated in real-time
d) Short term predicted use is computed from stored data for the previous 24-hour period, the typical day of the week usage and the forecasted ambient outdoor temperatures in each of the regions where the company distributes electricity
e) Measurement of the capacity of the power distribution network relative to demand and available power input resources to avoid brownouts or initiating blackouts to protect the network

Which of the above requirements are outside of the scope of Test Analyst's responsibilities (as specified in the Syllabus)?

Select TWO options

Question #35 (3 Points)

A customer is building a website using WordPress™. The website requires a number of software modules to perform standard tasks such as; spam filtering, layout and design theme and contact form. The contact form module is a standard code version which may be configured to provide a simple layout defining a message, various flags and some mandatory fields, such as email address and phone number. The requirements for testing the contact form module include:

i. Permitted format of an email address
ii. Permitted telephone number and area code formats
iii. National language and non-standard characters within the area for written text
iv. Recovery of the website following a server failure
v. Server email account securely transmits the contact form content via the WordPress email account

Which of the above requirements should the Test Analyst consider during test design?

a) i, ii, iii
b) iv, v
c) i, ii, iii, iv
d) i, v

Select ONE option

Question #36 (2 Points)

You are working on a mobile application for purchasing ladies' shoes online. The application has been designed with a high degree of usability and has been used successfully in the United Kingdom. The application is to be introduced into several European countries. During testing of the user interface, you are repeatedly having issues with truncated text on the buttons displayed. The UK shoe size standard used in product descriptions is one digit (size 2 to 9), European sizes are two digits (35 to 40). The translated text in some cases is longer in European languages compared to that in English. 'Buy Now' in English translates to 'Achetez Maintenant' in French and results in only 'Maintenant' (Now) appearing in place of 'Buy Now', leaving the user guessing how to proceed.

From the information above and the usability checklist below, which most likely has been overlooked in the user interface design sessions?

a) Definition of each field and its function
b) All user prompts defined and consistent
c) Screen layout matches specifications
d) Localisation requirements

Select ONE option

Question #37 (2 Points)

You have the following user story for a banking application. As an online user, I want to transfer cash from my current account easily as I never want to wait a long time to have money available to move into a savings account when I have seen a better interest rate.

Based on the user story checklist provided in the Syllabus, what is most incorrect with this user story?

a) More than one item of functionality
b) More than one main path
c) Dependencies on the availability of other accounts
d) Acceptance criteria are not testable

Select ONE option

Question #38 (2 Points)

You are a Test Analyst assigned to a project developing an updated application for an online grocery supplier. The company wants to encourage regular orders from its customers. A new component is to be integrated into the application to enable a delivery plan option. Customers will pay a fixed annual fee which entitles them to one free delivery a week. The specification allows for changes to delivery times and dates, to another UK address and amendments to a stored regular order. Changes to orders must be made no later than 24 hours before the time of delivery. You have the following user story:

User Story 1.2/20: Amend regular order under delivery plan scheme.
As a customer with a delivery plan, for one week only I want to change my order so that I can still receive deliveries at another location where service is provided.

Feature

Action	Acceptance Criteria
Login	Login is successful, system takes user to 'Check Regular Delivery Plan', verifies user has an established plan, retrieves the regular order and displays a defined set of options
Select 'Change Order'	System checks user's selection and takes user to the 'Make Changes' component. System prompts for type of change required
User inputs changes	'Make Changes' component checks the change and if the change is valid, makes the appropriate alteration to the order. System prompts for additional changes, continues as above until all required changes have been made. System displays all changes and prompts the user to submit the order
User submits order	System confirms order has been submitted successfully

You are reviewing the user story above with the following checklist:

a) Feature is clearly defined, distinct and consistent with the specification
b) Written from the view of the person who is requesting it
c) Acceptance criteria are defined and testable
d) Independent of any others
e) Follows commonly used format: As a < type of user >, I want < a goal > so that < a reason >

Which two from the checklist above are not achieved with this user story?

Select TWO options

Question #39 (2 Points)

You are working on a project where the decision has been made to use a key-word-driven automation tool. The following are required:

i. Creating the keyword/action word data
ii. Maintaining the keyword/action word data
iii. Writing the automation scripts
iv. Investigating any failures that may occur
v. Execution of the keyword-driven tests

In your role as Test Analyst, which of the tasks could you be expected to perform?

a) iii, iv, v
b) i, ii, iv, v
c) ii, iii, iv
d) i, ii, iii, v

Select ONE option

Question #40 (1 Point)

Using test tools, which of the following statements is most true?

a) Return on investment is usually lowest when automating regression tests
b) Tools for test execution are used during integration, system and acceptance testing
c) Return on investment for tools for test execution is usually lowest when automating regression tests and easiest to implement when based on documented low-level test cases
d) For comparisons, working out the expected result manually is often tedious and error-prone, it may be preferable to find or create an automated test oracle

Select ONE option

PRACTICE EXAM TWO ANSWERS

40 Answers

Question Number	Correct Answer	Learning Objective	K-Level	Points
1	b	TA-1.2.1	K2	1
2	a	TA-1.3.1	K2	1
3	b, d	TA-1.4.1	K2	1*
4	c	TA-1.4.2	K4	3
5	d	TA-1.4.2	K4	3
6	d	TA-1.5.1	K2	1
7	a	TA-2.1.1	K3	2
8	d	TA-3.2.1	K4	3
9	d	TA-3.2.2	K4	3
10	b	TA-3.2.3	K4	3
11	a	TA-3.2.3	K4	3
12	d	TA-3.2.4	K4	3
13	b	TA-3.2.4	K4	3
14	b	TA-3.2.5	K2	1
15	c	TA-3.2.6	K4	3
16	a	TA-3.2.6	K4	3
17	a, e	TA-3.2.7	K4	3*
18	c	TA-3.2.7	K4	3
19	b	TA-3.2.8	K4	3
20	b, e	TA-3.2.8	K4	3*
21	a, b	TA-3.3.1	K2	1*
22	a, c	TA-3.3.2	K3	2*
23	d	TA-3.3.3	K2	1
24	a, b	TA-3.4.1	K4	3*
25	c	TA-4.2.1	K2	1
26	c	TA-4.2.2	K2	1
27	c	TA-4.2.2	K2	1
28	c	TA-4.2.3	K2	1
29	a, b	TA-4.2.3	K2	1*
30	b	TA-4.2.4	K2	1
31	c	TA-4.2.5	K2	1
32	b, c	TA-4.2.5	K2	1*
33	c	TA-4.2.6	K2	1
34	b, e	TA-4.2.7	K4	3*
35	a	TA-4.2.7	K4	3
36	d	TA-5.2.1	K3	2
37	d	TA-5.2.2	K3	2
38	a, d	TA-5.2.2	K3	2*
39	b	TA-6.2.1	K3	2
40	d	TA-6.3.1	K2	1

* If both options selected are correct, the full number of points assigned to the question are awarded, otherwise no points are given.

Question	Correct Answer	Explanation / Rationale	Learning Objective K-Level	Points
Q1	b	b) is the correct answer. ii. and iv. are not true, this makes options a), c) and d) incorrect as they include one or both of these. Agile projects involve testing from the start. A much closer working relationship with stakeholders is common with Agile projects.	TA-1.2.1 K2	1
Q2	a	a) is the correct answer. iv. and v. are part of test design. All options other than a) include either iv. or v. making them incorrect.	TA-1.3.1 K2	1
Q3	b, d	b) and d) are the correct options. a) is not always true. Having a broad range of stakeholders is typically beneficial but this is not the same as having a large number. It is important stakeholders are the right ones. Having the wrong people involved may stand in the way of progress if there are other agendas, insufficient knowledge, fear of failure leading to inadvisable cautionary approaches or other reasons. b) is true. Having a broad range of stakeholders with different perspectives is likely to uncover and reduce risks. c) is not true. Input from Stakeholders can provide valuable knowledge such that requirements and constraints can be better specified. d) is true. Involving stakeholders means it is more likely the project will have a positive outcome. e) is not the best option as it may not be true. Stakeholders may have unrealistic expectations. Monitoring expectations and effective communication are required to ensure success.	TA-1.4.1 K2	1*
Q4	c	c) is the best approach. With automated testing is planned for the future, there is good documentation, a requirement to meet regulatory rules and no tight timescale, so low-level test cases are the best approach for i. iii. iv. and v. R2020-2 covers the requirement to display geofenced areas and dead zones which are subject to change and display of these areas alone would not be a regulatory requirement. Therefore, ii. would be best covered by high-level test cases.	TA-1.4.2 K4	3

Q5	d	d) is the correct answer. Low-level test cases are useful when the requirements are well-defined, the testers are less experienced and external verification of the tests, such as an audit, is required. Option a) is not the best option. This refers to high-level test cases, testers are domain experts without proper knowledge of formal testing and as independent verification of test is required, low-level testing is more appropriate. b) is not the best option. This refers to high-level test cases but low-level test cases provide a better basis for future automation of test cases. c) is not the best option. This refers to high-level test cases and traceability as a fundamental requirement. Reproducibility for audit verification is best done with low-level test cases.	TA-1.4.2 K4	3
Q6	d	d) is the correct answer as it has appropriate actions to cover all the problems. a) is not the best option as the problems with tests 2 and 5 could be incorrect documentation. Test 4 has already been resolved as a typographical error so there is no need to repeat the test. b) is not the best option as the specification has not been checked to confirm the expected result has been correctly entered in the log. There is no problem indicated with test 3. Test 4 has already been resolved as a typographical error. c) is not the best option as it does include addressing the problem with test 5. Test 4 has already been resolved as a typographical error.	TA-1.5.1 K2	1
Q7	a	a) is the most appropriate answer. Risk assessment is the process of identifying and subsequently analysing the identified project or product risk to determine its level of risk. Risk mitigation tasks include recognising new risks identified by information obtained during testing and also re-evaluating known issues based on relevant additional information. Risk identification is the process of identifying risks using techniques such as brainstorming, checklists and failure history. Prioritising tests is done by assessing both the impact and likelihood of a defect occurring.	TA-2.1.1 K3	2

<table>
<tr><td>Q8</td><td>d</td><td>d) is the correct answer. There are six partitions to test, the five shown in the table and an additional partition below £1 as from the scenario, an error is required for a purchase price of less than £1. a) is missing a test for above £1.5m. b) is missing a test for the partition £125,001 to £250,000. c) is missing a test for the partition covering less than £1.</td><td>TA-3.2.1
K4</td><td>3</td></tr>
<tr><td>Q9</td><td>d</td><td>d) is the correct answer. This covers all the boundaries with two-value coverage. The boundaries to consider are 1, 12, 24 and max sessions.</td><td>TA-3.2.2
K4</td><td>3</td></tr>
<tr><td>Q10</td><td>b</td><td>b) is the correct answer.
For a collapsed table start with a decision table covering combinations of conditions:
<table>
<tr><th>Test Case</th><th>1</th><th>2</th><th>3</th><th>4</th><th>5</th><th>6</th><th>7</th><th>8</th><th>9</th><th>10</th><th>11</th><th>12</th><th>13</th><th>14</th><th>15</th><th>16</th></tr>
<tr><td>Condition</td><td></td><td></td><td></td><td></td><td></td><td></td><td></td><td></td><td></td><td></td><td></td><td></td><td></td><td></td><td></td><td></td></tr>
<tr><td>80% attendance?</td><td>Y</td><td>Y</td><td>Y</td><td>Y</td><td>Y</td><td>Y</td><td>Y</td><td>Y</td><td>N</td><td>N</td><td>N</td><td>N</td><td>N</td><td>N</td><td>N</td><td>N</td></tr>
<tr><td>3 essays ≥5?</td><td>Y</td><td>Y</td><td>Y</td><td>Y</td><td>N</td><td>N</td><td>N</td><td>N</td><td>Y</td><td>Y</td><td>Y</td><td>Y</td><td>N</td><td>N</td><td>N</td><td>N</td></tr>
<tr><td>2 essays ≥8?</td><td>Y</td><td>Y</td><td>N</td><td>N</td><td>Y</td><td>Y</td><td>N</td><td>N</td><td>Y</td><td>Y</td><td>N</td><td>N</td><td>Y</td><td>Y</td><td>N</td><td>N</td></tr>
<tr><td>Exam taken?</td><td>Y</td><td>N</td><td>Y</td><td>N</td><td>Y</td><td>N</td><td>Y</td><td>N</td><td>Y</td><td>N</td><td>Y</td><td>N</td><td>Y</td><td>N</td><td>Y</td><td>N</td></tr>
<tr><td>Action</td><td></td><td></td><td></td><td></td><td></td><td></td><td></td><td></td><td></td><td></td><td></td><td></td><td></td><td></td><td></td><td></td></tr>
<tr><td>Sit exam</td><td>Y</td><td>Y</td><td>Y</td><td>Y</td><td>Y</td><td>Y</td><td>N</td><td>N</td><td>Y</td><td>N</td><td>Y</td><td>N</td><td>Y</td><td>N</td><td>N</td><td>N</td></tr>
</table>
If an exam has been taken in another faculty, attendance of 80% or more is not required for taking this exam so attendance can be replaced by ~. If attendance is 80% and one of the coursework conditions is met, it doesn't matter if an exam has been taken at another faculty, so the latter can be marked with a ~. If one of the coursework conditions is met, the exam cannot be taken regardless of attendance being 80% and an exam has been taken in another faculty. In this case, the latter two can both be marked with ~. Only one of the coursework conditions being 'Yes', is required, the other can be replaced by ~. For neither attendance 80% nor exam at another faculty, the student cannot sit the exam regardless of coursework.</td><td>TA-3.2.3
K4</td><td>3</td></tr>
</table>

Test Case	1	2	3	4	5	6	7	8	9	10	11	12	13	14	15	16
Condition																
80% attendance?	~	Y	~	Y	~	Y	~	~	~	N	~	N	~	N	~	~
3 essays ≥5?	Y	Y	Y	Y	~	~	N	N	Y	Y	Y	~	~	~	N	N
2 essays ≥8?	~	~	~	~	Y	Y	N	N	~	~	~	~	Y	~	N	N
Exam taken?	Y	~	Y	~	Y	~	~	~	Y	N	Y	N	Y	N	~	~
Action																
Sit exam	Y	Y	Y	Y	Y	Y	N	N	Y	N	Y	N	Y	N	N	N

Collapse column 4 into 2, collapse 8, 15 and 16 into 7, collapse 12 and 14 into 10, collapse 3, 9 and 11 into 1, and 13 into 5.

Test Case	1	2	5	6	7	10
Condition						
80% attendance?	~	Y	~	Y	~	N
3 essays ≥5?	Y	Y	~	~	N	~
2 essays ≥8?	~	~	Y	Y	N	~
Exam taken?	Y	~	Y	~	~	N
Action						
Sit exam	Y	Y	Y	Y	N	N

This leaves six test cases.

Using Inspection:
From the scenario, 6 test cases are needed for:
Exam can be sat:
1 Attendance 80%, 3 essays ≥5,
2 Attendance 80%, 2 essays ≥8,
3 Exam other faculty, 3 essays ≥5,
4 Exam taken in other faculty 2 essays ≥8.
Exam not allowed:
5 Attendance 80%, no exam in another facility,
6 No coursework completed.

Decision table covering individual condition outcomes:
With all four conditions having one of two values, individual condition outcomes can be achieved in 4 + 1 = 5 test cases.

This makes b) the correct answer, (6 - 5)

Question	Answer	Explanation	Learning Objective	Points
Q11	a	a) is the correct answer.	TA-3.2.3 K4	3

OED definition method:
With 3 options for condition 1 (three ticket types; **A**dult, **S**tudent, **C**hild), two options for each of condition 2 (Monday or not) and condition 3 (Promo or not) the full decision table covering all combinations where a ticket is purchased needs 12 (3 x 2 x 2) columns. For the first two weeks, no columns can be collapsed.

Test Case	**1**	**2**	**3**	**4**	**5**	**6**	**7**	**8**	**9**	**10**	**11**	**12**
Condition												
Ticket?	A	S	C	A	S	C	A	S	C	A	S	C
Monday?	Y	Y	Y	Y	Y	Y	N	N	N	N	N	N
Promo?	Y	Y	Y	N	N	N	Y	Y	Y	N	N	N
Action												
£Price	20	10	6	20	10	6	20	10	6	20	10	6
£Discount	10	5	3	10	5	3	0	0	0	0	0	0
Promo £1	1	1	1	0	0	0	1	1	1	0	0	0
£Outcome	**9**	**4**	**2**	**10**	**5**	**3**	**19**	**9**	**5**	**20**	**10**	**6**

For the last two weeks, the first three columns are no longer required, leaving nine columns.

Test Case	**1**	**2**	**3**	**4**	**5**	**6**
Condition						
Ticket?	A	S	C	A	S	C
Monday?	Y	N	Y	N	Y	N
Action						
£Price	20	10	6	20	10	6
£Discount	10	0	3	0	5	0
£Outcome	**10**	**10**	**9**	**20**	**5**	**6**

Conditions with 2 values (and method used in ISTQB Sample Exam, question #11)

C1 Adult ticket (Yes/No)
C2 Student ticket (Yes/No)
C3 Monday? (Yes/No)
C4 Promo code (Yes/No)

A child's ticket is assumed when C1 and C2 are both No.

The number of columns required for the 4 two value conditions is 16 (2^4).

Test Case	1	2	3	4	5	6	7	8	9	10	11	12	13	14	15	16
Condition																
Adult?	Y	Y	Y	Y	Y	Y	Y	Y	N	N	N	N	N	N	N	N
Student?	Y	Y	Y	Y	N	N	N	N	Y	Y	Y	Y	N	N	N	N
Monday?	Y	Y	N	N	Y	Y	N	N	Y	Y	N	N	Y	Y	N	N
Promo?	Y	N	Y	N	Y	N	Y	N	Y	N	Y	N	Y	N	Y	N
Action																
£Price	30	30	30	30	20	20	20	20	10	10	10	10	0	0	0	0
£Discount	15	15	0	0	10	10	0	5	5	0	0	0				
Promo £1	1	0	1	0	1	0	1	0	1	0	1	0	1	0	1	0
£Outcome	**14**	**15**	**29**	**30**	**9**	**10**	**19**	**15**	**14**	**10**	**9**	**10**				

Columns 1, 2, 3 and 4 are non-feasible as a ticket cannot be both adult and student at the same time. This results in 12 columns. Columns 13, 14, 15 and 16 can be reassigned to Child ticket and completed as appropriate.

For the last two weeks, using C1, C2 and C3, a table with 8 (2^3) columns is required. But two columns will be non-feasible (where ticket is shown as both adult and student) leaving 6 columns. Two columns would also need to be reassigned to Child ticket.

Q12	d	d) is the correct answer. There are nine 1-switches: Activate – Acceptance – Activate Activate – Acceptance – Disputed Activate – Disputed – Activate Activate – Closure – Disputed Activate – Closure – Filing Activate – Activate – Activate Activate – Activate – Acceptance Activate – Activate – Closure Activate – Activate – Disputed	TA-3.2.4 K4	3
Q13	b	b) is the correct answer. The problem appears to happen with two transitions, which will be tested with 1-switch testing.	TA-3.2.4 K4	3
Q14	b	b) is the correct answer. Classification trees are a way to test constrained combinations of parameters. If the parameters fall into distinct, non-overlapping sets, equivalence partitioning can be used and then combinations of items from different sets can be chosen as nodes.	TA-3.2.5 K2	1

<table>
<tr>
<td>Q15</td>
<td>c</td>
<td>c) is the correct answer. The two parameters with the greatest number of values are Agent with four values and Protocol also with four values. The minimum number of test cases required is 16 (4 x 4). Options a) and b) are below the minimum number and are therefore incorrect. d) is a distractor.
<table>
<tr><th>Test Case</th><th>Platform</th><th>Agent</th><th>Protocol</th></tr>
<tr><td>1</td><td>Windows</td><td>User - admin</td><td>Browser Chrome</td></tr>
<tr><td>2</td><td>Windows</td><td>User - inspector</td><td>Browser Edge</td></tr>
<tr><td>3</td><td>Windows</td><td>User - owner</td><td>Browser Safari</td></tr>
<tr><td>4</td><td>Windows</td><td>Auto input</td><td>sftp</td></tr>
<tr><td>5</td><td>MacOS</td><td>User - admin</td><td>Browser Edge</td></tr>
<tr><td>6</td><td>MacOS</td><td>User - inspector</td><td>Browser Chrome</td></tr>
<tr><td>7</td><td>MacOS</td><td>User - owner</td><td>sftp</td></tr>
<tr><td>8</td><td>MacOS</td><td>Auto input</td><td>Browser Safari</td></tr>
<tr><td>9</td><td>Linux</td><td>User - admin</td><td>Browser Safari</td></tr>
<tr><td>10</td><td>Linux</td><td>User - inspector</td><td>sftp</td></tr>
<tr><td>11</td><td>Linux</td><td>User - owner</td><td>Browser Chrome</td></tr>
<tr><td>12</td><td>Linux</td><td>Auto input</td><td>Browser Edge</td></tr>
<tr><td>13</td><td>~</td><td>User - admin</td><td>sftp</td></tr>
<tr><td>14</td><td>~</td><td>User - inspector</td><td>Browser Safari</td></tr>
<tr><td>15</td><td>~</td><td>User - owner</td><td>Browser Edge</td></tr>
<tr><td>16</td><td>~</td><td>Auto input</td><td>Browser Chrome</td></tr>
</table>
For completeness, the 40 parameter-value pairs are:
Windows/User-admin, Windows/User-inspector, Windows/User-owner, Windows/Auto input
Windows/Browser-Chrome, Windows/Browser-Edge, Windows/Browser-Safari, Windows/sftp
Mac/User-admin, Mac/User-inspector, Mac/User-owner, Mac/Auto input
Mac/Browser-Chrome, Mac/Browser-Edge, Mac/Browser-Safari, Mac/sftp
Linux/User-admin, Linux/User-inspector, Linux/User-owner, Linux/Auto input
Linux/Browser-Chrome, Linux/Browser-Edge, Linux/Browser-Safari, Linux/sftp
User-admin/Browser Chrome, User-admin/Browser Edge, User-admin/Browser Safari, User-admin/sftp
User-inspector/Browser Chrome, User-inspector/Browser Edge, User-inspector/Browser Safari, User-inspector/sftp
User-owner/Browser Chrome, User-owner/Browser Edge, User-owner/Browser Safari, User-owner/sftp
Auto input/Browser Chrome, Auto input/Browser Edge, Auto input/Browser Safari, Auto input/sftp.</td>
<td>TA-3.2.6
K4</td>
<td>3</td>
</tr>
</table>

Q16	a	Answer b) is correct. There are four parameters, each with two values: Disc drive: SSD or HDD, Keyboard: Std or Ext'd, Graphics card: NVIDIA or AMD, Screen: 20" or 27" d) is the distractor as 24 is the total number of pairs to be tested. The guideline minimum number of rows for a pairwise table suggests 4 (2 x 2) rows (test cases). However, as there are more than three two value parameters, this is a scenario when the actual number of test cases required is greater than the guideline minimum. Scenarios with 4 to 7 parameters with two values should start with an orthogonal array of 8 rows and then drop rows that are not required, with the number of rows remaining being greater than the minimum guideline number. Being able to recall this, will lead to discarding options b), c) and d). Otherwise, example 3 in Chapter *Pairwise Testing* shows how to answer a question with four two value parameters using an orthogonal array. Alternatively, as the number of parameters is relatively small, this can be worked out manually following example 2 in Chapter *Pairwise Testing.*	TA-3.2.6 K4	3
Q17	a, e	a) and e) are the correct options. a) Testing all behaviours as shown in the two test cases may mask errors. If better diagnostic capability is required, one additional test per alternate behaviour may be required. b) is not true as the embedded exception 6.5 is not tested in either of the two test cases specified. c) is not the best answer as the user is wanting to select a small wash-basin, this should be the main path and not the exception at step 5. d) is not true as after step 6.5 there is no specification of what happens next. Step 6.3 should state, User selects 'Pop-up' for 6.3.1 to be correct.	TA-3.2.7 K4	3*
Q18	c	c) is the correct answer. The test cases needed are: 1, 2, 3, 4, 5 ,6, 7, 8, 9, 10, 11, 12, 13, 14 1, 2, E1, 3, 4, E2, 5, 6, 7, E3, 8, 9, E4, 10,11,12, E5,13,14 1, 2, 3, 4, E2, 14 1, 2, 3, 4, 5, 6, 7, 8, 9, E4, 14 1, 2, 3, 4, 5, 6, 7, 8, 9, 10, 11, 12, E5, 14	TA-3.2.7 K4	3

Q19	b	b) is the best answer. Although the cost of shipping depends on several factors, you have only been asked to test the handling of costs associated with weight. Mistakes, if there are any, may occur at the boundary values of the shipping cost rates. Using boundary value analysis provides this extra confidence compared to using equivalence partitioning or a classification tree. Decision tables would be more appropriate if testing all the factors (weight, size and destination) is required.	TA-3.2.8 K4	3
Q20	b, e	b) and e) are the correct answers. Option a) is not the best option. Although there is an existing system, there is no indication you have previously worked with this and the specification has detailed information making this is not one of the best options. b) is correct as a classification tree offers the opportunity to manage combinations of inputs effectively. c) is not the best option. The number of tiles to be removed for a particular wall fixing is defined and this results in detailed combinations of inputs making b) and e) better testing techniques. d) is not the best answer. While use case testing may be appropriate to the likely development approach but would be based more on overall functional flow than on detailed combinations of inputs. e) is correct. The inputs exist in partitions (options with the specified number of tiles to be removed).	TA-3.2.8 K4	3*
Q21	a, b	a) and b) are the correct options for a user interface taxonomy. The other options are not the most appropriate for a taxonomy for the usability of the user interface. c) is performance, d) is functionality/ calculation. e) is not user interface usability.	TA-3.3.1 K2	1*
Q22	a, c	a) and c) options are the 'not true' answers. a) is untrue as good exploratory testing is planned. c) is untrue as tools can be used that do not record the expected outcomes, as they do not capture the GUI interaction. In this situation, the expected outcomes must be noted down so that proper analysis of defects can be undertaken.	TA-3.3.2 K3	2*

Q23	d	d) is the correct answer as the statement is not true. a), b) and c) are all true. Defect-based testing derives tests from lists which focus on defects.	TA-3.3.3 K2	1
Q24	a, b	a) and b) are the correct options. Boundary value analysis will test the payment thresholds. Decision tables will consider the conditions such as 'valid loyalty card' and 'qualifying products'. c) is not the best option as equivalence partitioning would check transactions within certain bounds but as the defects are thought to be at the payment thresholds, boundary value analysis is more suitable. d) might provide some benefit, but as the defects are already documented, this is not the best technique. e) is not the best option as testing against a defect taxonomy is likely to take significant time and not be targeted specifically at areas suspected of causing the defects.	TA-3.4.1 K4	3*
Q25	c	c) is the correct answer. Usability is a specified requirement. Users have had very little involvement and as the update is intended to enhance the user experience, it is important to test functional appropriateness. a) is not the best answer as functional correctness is not the main focus because, in the software, it has been re-used from a version that has been in use for two years. There is no evidence that accuracy and correctness have been a problem. So there is low risk there will be problems with functional correctness in the new application. b) is incorrect. The sub-characteristic of compatibility that the Test Analyst is responsible for is interoperability. From the information available, interoperability is not a particular requirement making b) not the most appropriate. d) is not the most appropriate option as the application is based on a previous version with the new features being additive.	TA-4.2.1 K2	1
Q26	c	c) is the correct answer. a) is functional appropriateness b) includes 'testing verifies the application's adherence to the specified or implied requirements.' This is functional correctness. d) is not correct as it contains some of functional appropriateness, see a).	TA-4.2.2 K2	1

Q27	c	c) is the correct answer. Functional correctness includes computational accuracy and test cases 2, 3 and 4 involve calculation. Test Case 1 verifies 10% extra time will be sufficient for a longer route.	TA-4.2.2 K2	1
Q28	c	c) is the correct answer. Functional correctness can be conducted at any test level and includes verifying computational accuracy. Functional appropriateness testing includes evaluating the appropriateness of a set of functions for its intended specified tasks and is usually conducted during system testing (or the later stages of integration testing). Interoperability verifies the exchange of information between two or more systems and can be tested at integration level. Lower than expected levels of functional completeness is an indication that the system has not been fully implemented.	TA-4.2.3 K2	1
Q29	a, b	a) and b) are the correct options. Option c) is not the best option. Functional appropriateness testing is based on the functional design e.g. use cases and/or user stories but typically not decision tables which are more commonly used for functional correctness testing. d) is not the best answer as functional correctness is defined as the verification of adherence to the specified or implied requirements. e) is not the best answer as lower than expected levels of functional completeness indicate the system has not been fully implemented.	TA-4.2.3 K2	1*
Q30	b	b) is the correct answer. You have been brought onto the project as it has been noticed that there has been an issue with fewer uptakes by new users than expected Usability should be verified against the requirements and validated by prospective users as current users may now be familiar the software. There may be learnability issues with the updated user interface. a) is not the best option as the problem is not with experienced users. c) is not the best option as the users may not be prospective users. d) is incorrect as it is a load test. This is not a responsibility of a Test Analyst.	TA-4.2.4 K2	1

Q31	c	c) is the correct answer. iii. and v. are portability issues making the other options, which include one or both of these, incorrect.	TA-4.2.5 K2	1
Q32	b, c	b) and c) are the correct options. a) is not correct as it is installability. b) is correct. The application allows synchronous or asynchronous requests. If one of the external suppliers' system queues a response, in that time another supplier may have received the order. c) is correct. 'Product not available' is specified for where a product has been discontinued. It is not intended to be used for other situations where the product is not available. d) is not correct. The requesting system should have details, in a format it can use, of why the account has a hold on it. The requirements should specify the protocol to use. e) is not the best option, it is performance testing of the supplier's system.	TA-4.2.5 K2	1*
Q33	c	c) is the correct answer. Portability tests relate to the degree to which a software component or system can be transferred to its intended environment. Interoperability testing could be significant for a system based on the Internet of Things, making none of the other options containing v. the best answer.	TA-4.2.6 K2	1
Q34	b, e	b) and e) are the correct answers. Option b) is a fault-tolerance requirement, e) is a performance capacity requirement and both of these, according to the Syllabus are responsibilities of the Technical Test Analyst, not the T.A. a), c) and d) are functional suitability and are the responsibilities of the T. A.	TA-4.2.7 K4	3*
Q35	a	a) is the correct answer according to the Syllabus. iv. is an example of testing for recoverability, a sub-characteristic of reliability which is a responsibility of the Technical Test Analyst. v. is a security issue and is a responsibility if the Technical Test Analyst.	TA-4.2.7 K4	3
Q36	d	d) is the correct answer. Defects have arisen because the process of making the software local for other European countries has not been addressed. a) is not correct because the definition of the function of a field has not changed. b) is not the best answer as the user prompts are consistent if the full text is displayed. c) is not the best option as there is no information suggesting the screen layout needs to be changed.	TA-5.2.1 K3	2

Q37	d	d) is the correct answer. There is no detail on what is considered 'easy' or 'a long time' making this untestable. The requirement would be testable if it said, 'should conform to usability standards stated in the usability standards document and the response time should be no greater than 5 seconds.' Option a) is not correct as there is only one item of functionality, to withdraw the cash. b) is not correct as it applies to use cases and not user stories. c) is not correct as there is no dependency on the other bank accounts being accessible, the story requires the cash to be available.	TA-5.2.2 K3	2
Q38	a, d	a) and d) are the correct answers. a) is not achieved. The requirement that changes should be made at least 24 hours in advance is not included in the user story. b) is achieved, the story is written from the user's view. c) is achieved, although the exact detail of what is displayed and prompts are not defined, acceptance criteria in terms of the system's actions are included and testable. d) is not achieved. There is dependency on the regular delivery plan component being available for determining if the user is signed up to the delivery plan. e) is achieved, the commonly used format for a user story is used.	TA-5.2.1 K3	2*
Q39	b	b) is the correct answer. The developer usually writes the automation scripts (automation code) so iii. is not part of the Test Analyst's role. All the other options with iii. are incorrect. The Test Analyst usually has responsibility for investigating any failures that occur, making iv. a responsibility. If the Test Analyst is unable to determine the cause of failure, only then should the information be handed to either the Technical Test Analyst or the developer for further analysis.	TA-6.2.1 K3	2

Q40	d	d) is the correct answer. Note the inclusion of 'may'. Option a) is not correct as return on investment is usually highest when automating regression tests. Option b) is not the best answer. While tools for test execution are used during integration, system and acceptance testing, some tools, particularly API testing tools, may also be used in component testing. Option c) is not correct. Whilst it is likely to be easier to implement tools for automation when there are documented low-level test cases, the return on investment for tools for test execution is usually highest when automating regression tests because of the low level of maintenance expected.	TA-6.3.1 K2	1

* If both options selected are correct, the full number of points assigned to the question are awarded, otherwise no points are given.

BOOKING THE EXAM

You are ready to book the exam when you feel you meet the requirements of the Learning Objectives.

In the period of transition when there are two versions of the Syllabus (2012 and 2019), make sure you know which Syllabus your intended exam adheres to. The exam based on the Syllabus 2012 is three hours duration. The exam based on the Syllabus 2019 is two hours duration. On 4th February 2021 all English language 2012 Advanced Level Test Analyst and Technical Test Analyst syllabus exams will be withdrawn. On 4th August 2021 all non-English language 2012 Advanced Level Test Analyst syllabus exams will be withdrawn.

Extra time of 25% can be given for non-native language candidates and those with certain special needs. Extra time must be agreed with the test centre and officially documented in advance. Check the time required to complete this well in advance of the date of the exam.

If you have attended a training course, you may have the exam fee included in the price you paid for the course. This may include two attempts at the exam. Your instructor will provide you with details.

Exams may be taken at approved test centres or online at home. For example, online exams are available from ASTQB, the American Software Testing Qualifications Board Inc. which accepts world-wide bookings. Online exams are also provided by GASQ, the Global Association for Software Quality. When choosing an online exam, check first you have an environment that meets the requirements. Also check you can complete the set-up verification requirements and understand the role of the proctor. Refer to the appropriate exam provider's website for details.

Keep in mind, the ISTQB statement from the ATA Sample Exam Introduction, the '*sample questions should offer many ideas for the individual Member Boards on how to create good questions and appropriate answer sets for their examinations'*. ISTQB publish exam rules, structure and question formats that should be used by the Member Boards. So exam questions can differ between Member Boards.

At the time of publication, the total price of the exam (fee and applicable tax) can vary by up to 20% between different providers.

The exam may be booked independently through several channels:

ISTQB® has a list of exam providers
www.istqb.org/istqb-where-you-are/find-an-exam-provider.html

BCS® The Chartered Institute for IT
www.bcs.org/get-qualified/certifications-for-professionals/software-testing-certifications/

ASTQB® The American Software Testing Qualifications Board Inc.
astqb.org/

GASQ® The Global Association for Software Quality
www.gasq.org/en/

iSQI® The International Software Quality Institute Inc.
isqi.org/en/16-istqb-certified-tester-advanced-level-test-analyst.html

Local Member Boards by country
istqb.org/istqb-where-you-are/your-local-member-board.html

The iSQI® has, at the time of publication, a 2TRY offer where you pay an extra 25% for two attempts at the exam. Promotion codes and offers may be available through other channels.

Good luck with the exam.

REFERENCES

This book has used the versions of ISTQB® documents, available at time of publication, from the ISTQB® website, www.istqb.org, further details are given below.

Launch Documents

Release

ISTQB® MEDIA RELEASE Brussels, February 4, 2020
ISTQB® releases new Certified Tester: Advanced Level Syllabus (2019-1) Test Analyst (CTAL-TA)
https://www.istqb.org/documents/pr/ISTQB-PR_CTAL-TA-TTA-04-02.pdf

Syllabus

ISTQB® Certified Tester Advanced Level Syllabus Test Analyst Version 2019 v1.1 December 19, 2019
https://www.istqb.org/downloads/category/69-2019-advanced-level-test-analyst.html

Select Advanced Level Syllabus (2019-1) Test Analyst

Sample Exam Questions and Answers

Sample Exam - Questions ISTQB® Test Analyst Syllabus Advanced Level Exam ID: A Version 2019 1.0
https://www.istqb.org/downloads/category/69-2019-advanced-level-test-analyst.html

Select AL 2019 Sample Exam TA Questions

Select AL 2019 Sample Exam TA Answers

Exam Format and Information

ISTQB® Certified Tester Advanced Level Syllabus Exam Structure and Rules Test Analyst / Technical Test Analyst 2019 V1.1 19 Dec 2019
https://www.istqb.org/downloads/category/67-2019-advanced-level-general-files.html

Select Advanced Level TA and TTA Exam Structure and Rules v1.1

ISTQB® Exam Information - Public Version 2. 2018
https://www.istqb.org/downloads/category/74-general-files.html
Select Public Information on Exam Structures 2.0

ISTQB® Standard Glossary Documents

The online Glossary is updated from time to time. This book uses the (updated) online version which is currently based on Glossary v3.3 with updates made to June 2020. (The next release of the Glossary will include updates).

ISTQB® Standard Glossary of Terms used in Software Testing, version 3.3 (with updates)
https://glossary.istqb.org/en/search/
Select Search Advanced Options, Uncheck All / Check Advanced test Analyst 2019 / reports / All Terms in Syllabus

ISTQB® Release Notes Standard Glossary of Terms used in Software Testing Version v3.3 11th November 2019
https://www.istqb.org/downloads/glossary.html
Select ISTQB_Glossary-Release-Notes_V3.3

ISTQB® Release Notes Standard Glossary of Terms used in Software Testing Version v3.2 15th April 20189
https://www.istqb.org/downloads/glossary.html
Select ISTQB_Glossary-Release-Notes_V3.2

ISTQB® Glossary Web App User Guide V1.0 Version 1.0 26th February 2020
https://www.istqb.org/downloads/glossary.html
Select ISTQB_Glossary-User-Guide_V1.0

Standards

[ISO25010] ISO/IEC 25010 (2011) Systems and software engineering – Systems and software Quality Requirements and Evaluation (SQuaRE) System and software quality models Chapter 4.

[ISO26515] ISO/IEC 26515 (2018) Systems and software engineering – Developing information for users in an agile environment.

[ISO29119-4] ISO/IEC/IEEE 29119-4 Software and Systems Engineering – Software Testing – Part 4, Test Techniques, 2015.

[ISO 9241-210:2019] Ergonomics of human-system interaction — Part 210: Human-centred design for interactive systems.

Oxford English Dictionary
www.oed.com

Other Documents and Sources

ISTQB® Foundation Syllabus for Usability Testing Specialist: 2018
https://www.istqb.org/downloads/category/58-usability-testing-documents.html
Select Usability Testing Specialist FL Syllabus

ISTQB® Advanced Level Syllabus Test Analyst: 2012
https://www.istqb.org/downloads/category/72-2012-advanced-level-test-analyst.html
Select Advanced Level (2012) Test Analyst

Orthogonal Arrays
University of York's online resources
www.york.ac.uk/depts/maths/tables/orthogonal.htm

Decision Table Example from a Question in the RBCS Software training and Consultancy Advanced Test Analyst Course
rbcs-us.com/blog/decision-tables-and-testing/
Copyright © 2020 Rex Black Consulting Services. All Rights Reserved.

British Computing Society
www.bcs.org/get-qualified/certifications-for-professionals/software-testing-certifications/istqb-certified-tester-advanced-level-test-analyst/

Process Specification
iwww.cs.nott.ac.uk/~pszjds/teaching/archive/G52LSSLecture17.pdf
Dr Dario Landa-Silva University of Nottingham School of Computer Science.

A Dictionary of Computer Science
Andrew Butterfield, Gerard Ekembe Ngondi, Oxford University Press, 2016

APPENDIX A: DECISION TABLE EXAMPLE

Tables and Answer for Example 7 (from page 29)

ISTQB Sample Exam Question #11

'Consider the following specification for a train ticket application:

- *If you want to take a train after 9AM you get the ticket at the "Super-Saver" price.*
- *If you want to take a train before 6AM you get the ticket at a "Saver" price.*
- *At other times of the day you pay the standard price.*
- *If you have a Railcard you get a 25% rebate for all tickets except "Super Saver".*

Using decision table testing, how many test cases are required to cover all non-redundant and feasible decision rules?

a) 3 test cases
b) 8 test cases
c) 4 test cases
d) 5 test cases

Select ONE option'

Answer

Using OED Definition

Condition C1 can have three values, before 6am, 6am to 9am and after 9am. C2 is needed for Railcard Yes or No. This requires a table with 6 (3 x 2) columns.

Test Case	**1**	**2**	**3**	**4**	**5**	**6**
Condition						
C1 - Time	Before 6am	Before 6am	6am-9am	6am-9am	After 9am	After 9am
C2 - Railcard	Y	N	Y	N	Y	N
Action						
Saver ticket	Y	Y	N	N	N	N
Super-Saver ticket	N	N	N	N	Y	Y
Standard ticket	N	N	Y	Y	N	N
25% discount	Y	N	Y	N	N	N

There are no columns that need dropping for non-feasible combinations. There is redundancy with column 6 as the actions don't change with or without a Railcard. Column 6 can be collapsed into column 5, with ~ replacing the Railcard entry.

Test Case	**1**	**2**	**3**	**4**	**5**
Condition					
C1 - Time	Before 6am	Before 6am	6am-9am	6am-9am	After 9am
C2 - Railcard	Y	N	Y	N	~
Action					
Saver ticket	Y	Y	N	N	N
Super-Saver ticket	N	N	N	N	Y
Standard ticket	N	N	Y	Y	N
25% discount	Y	N	Y	N	N

Using ISTQB definition

With the definition that a condition can have values, 'True' or 'False', the following complete decision table covers all combinations. Y (Yes) is used for true, N (No) is used for false. With four conditions, the table requires 16 (2^4) columns.

Test Case	**1**	**2**	**3**	**4**	**5**	**6**	**7**	**8**	**9**	**10**	**11**	**12**	**13**	**14**	**15**	**16**
Condition																
Before 6am?	Y	Y	Y	Y	Y	Y	Y	Y	N	N	N	N	N	N	N	N
6am-9am?	Y	Y	Y	Y	N	N	N	N	Y	Y	Y	Y	N	N	N	N
After 9am?	Y	Y	N	N	Y	Y	N	N	Y	Y	N	N	Y	Y	N	N
Railcard?	Y	N	Y	N	Y	N	Y	N	Y	N	Y	N	Y	N	Y	N
Action																
Saver ticket	Y	Y	Y	Y	Y	Y	Y	Y	N	N	N	N	N	N	N	N
Super-Saver ticket	Y	Y	N	N	Y	Y	N	N	Y	Y	N	N	Y	Y	N	N
Standard ticket	Y	Y	Y	Y	N	N	N	N	Y	Y	Y	Y	N	N	N	N
25% discount	Y	N	Y	N	Y	N	Y	N	N	N	Y	N	N	N	Y	N

This table above contains all possible combinations, regardless of whether or not they are feasible or redundant. Purchasing one ticket means non-feasible combinations occur in columns 1, 2, 3, 4, 5, 6, 9, 10, 15, 16. As a Railcard does not alter the outcome in columns 13 or 14, these can be collapsed into one column.

Test Case							**7**	**8**			**11**	**12**	**13**			
Condition																
Before 6am?							Y	Y			N	N	N			
6am-9am?							N	N			Y	Y	N			
After 9am?							N	N			N	N	Y			
Railcard?							Y	N			Y	N	~			
Action																
Saver ticket							Y	Y			N	N	N			
Super-Saver ticket							N	N			N	N	Y			
Standard ticket							N	N			Y	Y	N			
25% discount							Y	N			Y	N	N			

Adapting the ISTQB definition / used in the ISTQB Sample Answers

Condition C1: 'Before 6am, True or False?'

Condition C2: 'After 9am, True or False?'

The third option for a ticket '6am to 9am' is not set as a condition, it is assumed for when both C1 and C2 are 'False'

Condition 3 is 'Railcard True or False?'

With three conditions, each with two values, the decision table covering all combinations requires 8 (2^3) columns.

Test Case	**1**	**2**	**3**	**4**	**5**	**6**	**7**	**8**
Condition								
Before 6am?	Y	Y	Y	Y	N	N	N	N
After 9am?	Y	Y	N	N	Y	Y	N	N
Railcard?	Y	N	Y	N	Y	N	Y	N
Action								
Saver ticket	Y	Y	Y	Y	N	N	N	N
Super-Saver ticket	Y	Y	N	N	Y	Y	N	N
25% discount	Y	N	Y	N	N	N	Y	N

Columns 7 and 8 have both C1 and C2 set to 'N'. In this scenario, these columns are reassigned to the condition for a standard ticket. The assumption has been made that there is no requirement to test for no ticket being bought. In some scenarios, testing a combination of two N (No) with one Y (Yes) (columns 7) and three 'N's (column 8) may be valid and columns cannot then be reassigned.

If this scenario had included a further condition such as 'Parking in a nearby designated location', with a discount if a ticket is purchased or a Railcard is held, it would not be possible to reassign columns.

As it is not feasible to have both a Super-Saver and a Saver ticket for the same journey, columns 1 and 2 can be dropped. The reassigned columns 7 and 8 can be collapsed into one column as a railcard does not apply for a standard ticket.

Test Case			3	4	5	6	7	
Condition								
Before 6am?			Y	Y	N	N	N	
After 9am?			N	N	Y	Y	N	
Railcard?			Y	N	Y	N		
Action								
Saver ticket			Y	Y	N	N	N	
Super-Saver ticket			N	N	Y	Y	N	
25% discount			Y	N	N	N	Y	

In this approach, the full table cannot be considered as covering all combinations of conditions with the combinations including those of 'no ticket with no Railcard' and 'no ticket with a Railcard' as those columns are now representing a ticket between 6am and 9am. Arguably, this is reasonable in this scenario. But equally, the table includes other non-feasible test cases in columns 1 and 2, a ticket cannot be purchased before 6am and at the same time after 9am. For a consistent approach to non-feasible combinations, the method using the OED definition is a better approach.

BEWARE This method of omitting a condition value can be used here because the effect of having a Railcard is linked to having a ticket. There is no action for having a Railcard without a ticket. However, consider a scenario where a user can park at the train station for a pickup or other reason. If this replaces Railcard, so the third condition is 'Car Parking Yes/No', with a discount on tickets if purchased, it is now no longer possible to reassign the two columns as it is valid to park with no train ticket. So, if using the method of reassigning columns, be sure the conditions are not fully independent.

Summary

If the exam question #11 had asked the same question as in ISTQB Sample Exam question #10 '*What is the MINIMUM number of test cases to cover the full decision table?'* The answer, (6, 16 or 8) varies according to the definition of condition used.

However, the question asked, '*How many test cases are required to test all non-redundant and feasible decision rules?*' This requires a collapsed table. In this scenario, the columns collapsed are 1 for OED, 11 for ISTQB and 3 for adapted ISTQB methods. For all of these, the eventual table collapses to 5 columns.

d) is the correct answer.

APPENDIX B: USING ORTHOGONAL ARRAYS

Using Orthogonal Arrays for Pairwise Testing (pages 43-46)
Orthogonal arrays are most useful when there are a large number of parameters and/or a large number of parameter-values.

Determine the number of parameters and parameter values, then select an appropriate array from the Taguchi Designs Table below or another reliable source. Tables showing a larger number of parameters are available from various sources such as the University of York's online resources, see *References* Section.

If the array chosen can accommodate more columns than parameters, the extra columns can be dropped. If the array can accommodate more parameters or parameter-values than required, after mapping, on inspection it may be possible to reduce the rows due to duplication of pairs.

An additional column for the guideline minimum number of rows has been added to the table below which allows comparisons to be made.

Taguchi Designs Table

Array	Parameters and Values	Maximum Number of Rows that may be required	Number of Rows from method to calculate minimum number
L4 2^3	up to 3 parameters with 2 values each	4	4
L8 2^7	up to 7 parameters with 2 values each	8	4*
L12 2^11	up to 11 parameters with 2 values each	12	4*
L16 2^15	up to 15 parameters with 2 values each	16	4*
L32 2^31	up to 31 parameters with 2 values each	32	4*
L64 2^63	up to 63 parameters with 2 values each	64	4*
L9 3^4	up to 4 parameters with 3 values each	9	9
L27 3^13	up to 13 parameters with 3 values each	27	9*
L16' 4^5	up to 5 parameters with 4 values each	16	16
L25 5^6	6 parameters with 5 values each	25	25
L18 2^1 x 3^7	one parameter with 2 values and up to 7 parameters with 3 values each	18	4*
L36 2^3 x 3^13	up to 3 parameters with 2 values and up to 13 parameters with 3 values each.	36	9*
L36' 2^11 x 3^12	up to 11 parameters with 2 values and up to 12 parameters with 3 values each	36	9*
L32' 2^1 x 4^9	one parameter with 2 values and up to 9 parameters with 4 values each.	32	16*
L50 2^1 x 5^11	one parameter with 2 values and up to 11 parameters with 5 values each	50	25*

* The number indicated will not provide adequate test cases to cover all parameter-value pairs.

Tables showing a larger number of parameters are available from various sources such as the University of York's online resources: www.york.ac.uk/depts/maths/tables/orthogonal.htm. These tables are often called Taguchi Designs or Taguchi Tables.

Orthogonal Array Examples

L4 2^3.

	1	2	3
1	1	1	1
2	1	2	2
3	2	1	2
4	2	2	1

L8 2^7.

	1	2	3	4	5	6	7
1	1	1	1	1	1	1	1
2	1	1	1	2	2	2	2
3	1	2	2	1	1	2	2
4	1	2	2	2	2	1	1
5	2	1	2	1	2	1	2
6	2	1	2	2	1	2	1
7	2	2	1	1	2	2	1
8	2	2	1	2	1	1	2

L9 3^4.

	1	2	3	4
1	1	1	1	1
2	1	2	2	1
3	1	3	3	3
4	2	1	2	3
5	2	2	3	1
6	2	3	1	2
7	3	1	3	2
8	3	2	1	3
9	3	3	2	1

L16 4^5

	1	2	3	4	5
1	1	1	1	1	1
2	1	2	2	2	2
3	1	3	3	3	3
4	1	4	4	4	4
5	2	1	2	3	4
6	2	2	1	4	3
7	2	3	4	1	2
8	2	4	3	2	1
9	3	1	3	4	2
10	3	2	4	3	1
11	3	3	1	2	4
12	3	4	2	1	3
13	4	1	4	2	3
14	4	2	3	1	4
15	4	3	2	4	1
16	4	4	1	3	2

Worked Example
Parameters with their parameter values are:
Car: Salon (1), Hatchback (2)
Fuel: Diesel (1), Petrol (2), Electric (3)
Paint finish: Silver metallic (1), Red (2), black (3)
Interior: Black leather (1), Grey cloth (2), Multi-brown tweed (3)
Tyres: All-weather (1), Winter (2), Regular (3)

Four parameters with three parameter-values, 1 parameter with 2 parameter-values. From the table, this requires an L18 2^1 x 3^7 array. This is available from www.york.ac.uk/depts/maths/tables/l18.gif.

	Column / Parameter							
Test Case	**1**	**2**	**3**	**4**	**5**	**6**	**7**	**8**
1	1	1	1	1	1	1	1	1
2	1	1	2	2	2	2	2	2
3	1	1	3	3	3	3	3	3
4	1	2	1	1	2	2	3	3
5	1	2	2	2	3	3	1	1
6	1	2	3	3	1	1	2	2
7	1	3	1	2	1	3	1	1
8	1	3	2	3	2	1	3	1
9	1	3	3	1	3	2	1	2
10	2	1	1	3	3	2	2	1
11	2	1	2	1	1	3	3	2
12	2	1	3	2	2	1	1	3
13	2	2	1	2	3	1	3	2
14	2	2	2	3	1	2	1	3
15	2	2	3	1	2	3	2	1
16	2	3	1	3	2	3	1	2
17	2	3	2	1	3	1	2	3
18	2	3	3	2	1	2	3	1

Map the car parameter-values onto column 1 as this column has numbers 1 and 2 only. Map the other four parameters onto columns 2, 3, 4 and 5 as they have numbers 1, 2 and 3. Drop remaining columns.

	Parameter				
Test Case	**Car**	**Fuel**	**Paint**	**Interior**	**Tyres**
1	Saloon	Diesel	Silver	Cream	All-weather
2	Saloon	Diesel	Red	Grey	Winter
3	Saloon	Diesel	Black	Brown	Regular
4	Saloon	Petrol	Silver	Cream	Winter
5	Saloon	Petrol	Red	Grey	Regular
6	Saloon	Petrol	Black	Brown	All-weather
7	Saloon	Electric	Silver	Grey	All-weather
8	Saloon	Electric	Red	Brown	Winter
9	Saloon	Electric	Black	Cream	Regular
10	Hatchback	Diesel	Silver	Brown	Regular
11	Hatchback	Diesel	Red	Cream	All-weather
12	Hatchback	Diesel	Black	Grey	Winter
13	Hatchback	Petrol	Silver	Grey	Regular
14	Hatchback	Petrol	Red	Brown	All-weather
15	Hatchback	Petrol	Black	Cream	Winter
16	Hatchback	Electric	Silver	Brown	Winter
17	Hatchback	Electric	Red	Cream	Regular
18	Hatchback	Electric	Black	Grey	All-weather

Inspect the table for duplicate pairs and amend the table accordingly. This results in the table below:

	Parameter				
Test Case	**Car**	**Fuel**	**Paint**	**Interior**	**Tyres**
1	Saloon	Diesel	Silver	Cream	All-weather
2	Saloon	Diesel	Red	Grey	Winter
3	Saloon	Diesel	Black	Brown	Regular
4	Saloon	Petrol	Silver	Cream	Winter
5					
6					
7	Saloon	Electric	Silver	Grey	All-weather
8		Electric	Red	Brown	Winter
9		Electric	Black	Cream	Regular
10	Hatchback	Diesel	Silver	Brown	Regular
11	Hatchback		Red	Cream	All-weather
12	Hatchback			Grey	Winter
13	Hatchback	Petrol	Silver	Grey	Regular
14	Hatchback	Petrol	Red	Brown	All-weather
15	Hatchback	Petrol	Black		Winter
16					
17			Red		Regular
18			Black	Grey	All-weather

All the pairs in rows 5, 6 and 16 are covered elsewhere in the table, so these rows can be removed. The pairs in rows 12 and rows 15 can be put into one row. This leaves 14 rows, which equates to 14 tests, see table on next page:

	Parameter				
Test Case	**Car**	**Fuel**	**Paint**	**Interior**	**Tyres**
1	Saloon	Diesel	Silver	Cream	All-weather
2	Saloon	Diesel	Red	Grey	Winter
3	Saloon	Diesel	Black	Brown	Regular
4	Saloon	Petrol	Silver	Cream	Winter
5					
6					
7	Saloon	Electric	Silver	Grey	All-weather
8	~	Electric	Red	Brown	Winter
9	~	Electric	Black	Cream	Regular
10	Hatchback	Diesel	Silver	Brown	Regular
11	Hatchback	~	~	Cream	All-weather
12	Hatchback	Petrol	Black	Grey	Winter
13	Hatchback	Petrol	Silver	Grey	Regular
14	Hatchback	Petrol	Red	Brown	All-weather
15					
16					
17	Hatchback	Electric	Red		Regular
18	~	~	Black	Grey	All-weather

The 78 parameter-value pairs are tested with 14 test cases:

Hatchback/Diesel, Hatchback/Petrol, Hatchback/Electric, Hatchback/Black, Hatchback/Silver, Hatchback/Red, Hatchback/Brown, Hatchback/Cream, Hatchback/Grey, Hatchback/Regular, Hatchback/All-weather, Hatchback/Winter

Diesel/Black, Diesel/Silver, Diesel/Red, Diesel/Brown, Diesel/Cream, Diesel/Grey, Diesel/Regular, Diesel/Winter, Diesel/All-weather

Petrol/Black, Petrol/Silver, Petrol/Red, Petrol/Brown, Petrol/Cream, Petrol/Grey, Petrol/Regular, Petrol/Winter, Petrol/All-weather

Electric/Black, Electric/Silver, Electric/Red, Electric/Brown, Electric/Cream, Electric/Grey, Electric/Regular, Electric/Winter, Electric/All-weather

Black/Brown, Black/Cream, Black/Grey, Black/Regular, Black/Winter, Black/All-weather

Silver/Brown, Silver/Cream, Silver/Grey, Silver/Regular, Silver/Winter, Silver/All-weather

Red/Brown, Red/Cream, Red/Grey, Red/Regular, Red/winter, Red/All-weather

Brown/Regular, Brown/Winter, Brown/All-weather

Cream/Regular, Cream/Winter, Cream/All-weather

Grey/Regular, Grey/Winter, Grey/All-weather

QUOTATIONS

From the World of Software Testing

“Quality is never an accident; it is always the result of intelligent effort.” — John Ruskin

“Just because you’ve counted all the trees doesn’t mean you’ve seen the forest.” — Anonymous

“Software testers always go to heaven; they’ve already had their fair share of hell.” — Anonymous

“All code is guilty until proven innocent.” — Anonymous

“The bitterness of poor quality remains long after the sweetness of low price is forgotten.”— Benjamin Franklin

“Be a yardstick of quality. Some people aren’t used to an environment where excellence is expected.”— Steve Jobs

Q: “How many testers does it take to change a lightbulb?” A: “None, they just tell you that the room is dark.”— Anonymous

“Software and cathedrals are much the same: first we build them, then we pray.”— Anonymous

“Walking on water and developing software from a specification are easy if both are frozen.”— Edward V. Berard, American software engineer and consultant for The Object Agency, Inc.

“He who thinks a tool can solve all problems has a new problem.”— Federico Toledo, Co-founder Abstracta

“We have as many testers as we have developers. And testers spend all their time testing and developers spend half their time testing. We’re more of a testing, a quality software organization than we’re a software organization.”— Bill Gates

“Where is the ‘Any’ key?” Homer Simpson, trying to figure out the “Press Any Key” notification.

“Irreproducible bugs become highly reproducible right after delivery to the customer.”— Michael Stahl’s derivative of Murphy’s Law.

“A software bug costs a dollar to fix in-house, ten dollars in testing and a hundred in the field.” — Anonymous, often used by James G. Treybig Founder and CEO of Tandem Computers Inc.

Made in United States
North Haven, CT
05 November 2026

21760266R00115